FOLLOWING JESUS IN A POLITICALLY DIVIDED WORLD

An Interactive Guide to
21 Questions on
Christianity and Politics

JOHN WHITTAKER
& DANIEL MCCOY

a renew.org resource

So grateful for this book. John and Daniel succeeded in bringing this hot button topic to us in a way that engages the current political climate through the biblical lens of truth. We are encouraged to engage in politics to bring the kingship of Jesus to the world while describing the realistic expectations that believers should have in a fallen world. I'm encouraged to have this resource to help guide me and those I disciple in this politically charged culture.

—**Michelle Eagle**, Discipleship and Women's Minister, Harpeth Christian Church, co-author of *Identity: Who You Really Are in Christ*

I heartily recommend this book. Church leaders: if we don't disciple our people on how to think biblically about politics and elections, the world will. So, let's be fearless and use a book like this to teach our people how to think biblically about these important issues.

—**Bobby Harrington**, Lead Pastor, Harpeth Christian Church; CEO of RENEW.org and Discipleship.org

This short read offers a fantastic and practical guide that will help you navigate some of the difficult challenges we Christians face when engaging politics. Not only do the authors tackle some difficult questions; they provide the reader with a framework for discovering their own answers to those difficult questions. I recommend this book to anyone who is willing to think outside of the box and make the effort to discover what following Jesus looks like in every aspect of life, even the voting booth.

—**Paul Huyghebaert**, pastor, communicator, and author of *The Way Back: Repentance, the Presence of God, and the Revival the Church So Desperately Needs*

This is a compelling and much-needed resource as we find ourselves in a deeply divided political world. It is a timely reminder that through the grace of King Jesus we can lean into the issues around us, but we must love well. We are reminded by Daniel and John that our biblical theology must be our firm foundation and lens through which we view the crucial questions and issues of our day.

—**Andrew Jit**, Founder of MiT Global

There are plenty of voices in our culture telling us what to think. Instead, Daniel and John usher readers to many of the ethical crossroads of our day, offering a framework so that we may personally build biblical convictions as disciples of Jesus.

—**Jason Ishmael**, Lead Pastor, Antioch Christian Church

"Are you an American who happens to be a Christian, or a Christian who happens to live in America?" Daniel and John equip Christians to translate our confession into practical action within our unique social and political context. As someone entrusted with overseeing a local congregation, I would be thrilled to see this resource in the hands of my members.

—**Jaron Scott**, Lead Pastor, Christ's Church of Joplin; Professor of Organizational Leadership, Ozark Christian College

Following Jesus in a Politically Divided World is a timely resource to help believers think and behave Christianly when it comes to politics. Each short chapter includes practical, biblical steps for considering the polarizing issues of our day through a Jesus lens. With an abundance of biblical references and relevant examples from history, this is a perfect book for small group and classroom discussions. At a time when consequential issues are tearing us apart, the authors offer a process for reflection and engagement with Scripture to bridge our political divides while remaining faithful to the gospel and the mission of the church.

—**Matt Stafford**, Worship and Creative Arts Director, Ozark Christian College

As the church becomes increasingly discipled by competing political interests, the worship of the donkey and elephant has distracted many Christians from worshipping the Lamb. We need guidance on how to walk by faith in such anxious seasons. John Whittaker and Daniel McCoy have written a book that is thoughtful and accessible. Rather than persuading us to participate in a particular way, they help us to ask better questions about how to critically engage political topics and how to faithfully interact with government interests. This book is carefully researched, fair, and timely. If you only take one book into the ballot box with you this year, take the Bible. But if you take two, include this one.

—**Bob Turner**, Lead Minister, White Station Church of Christ

As I have matured in my faith and dedicated myself to understanding God's Word as the foundation for every action, conviction, and decision in my life, I have found myself drifting away from a blind allegiance to a particular political party. This shift has often created a tension in my identity as a Christian American. I suspect that many others who prioritize their citizenship in the Kingdom of God experience a similar struggle, and this book offers a timely and much-needed solution.

It presents biblical truths alongside a framework for evaluating our political views through the lens of God's character. *Following Jesus in a Politically Divided World* provides practical strategies for leading with love and standing firm in truth as we engage with others in a politically charged society. It equips us to navigate the complexities of a divisive culture and make informed choices that impact our world, including our decisions at the ballot box.

—**Tina Wilson**, author of *Step into Scripture: A Daily Journey to Understanding Your Bible*

CONTENTS

INTRODUCTION
IS IT POSSIBLE TO ENGAGE POLITICS
AND STILL LOVE EACH OTHER WELL?

Imagine being a church leader who watched the video of George Floyd's death in 2020 and then decided to host some conversations at church around issues of racial injustice. Then imagine having half your church respond to those conversations by crying, "Critical Race Theory!" and then leaving.

Wait . . . what?

Just because a conversation about race includes statements like, "My skin color alone can invoke fear in some people," and lamentations on the "silence about racial matters in the church" doesn't mean that somebody's gone "woke" or is promoting CRT from the pulpit. Those two quotes come directly from the most eye-opening conversation about race I (Daniel) have ever had, immediately following George Floyd's death, in which I learned a ton from a wise brother in Christ for whom the hurt was real and reopened. Cries against racism or "a particular vitriol that exists within our country toward black men" (again, my friend's words) don't make someone a progressive.

They might mean simply that a Christian hasn't closed their eyes to present hurt.

An opposite error is just as easy to make. Imagine being a church leader concerned about cultural trends coming on as fast as a terrain-transforming tsunami. Gender is something we construct based on feelings? Masculinity equals toxicity? Whiteness equals racism? When it comes to marriage, my church's position on marriage is homophobic? Our position on church leadership is misogynistic? Our position on Christian missions is imperialistic?

Sheesh, you might think. *Our nation has done precisely what Soviet dissident Solzhenitsyn once warned us about. We've forgotten God.* So, imagine that you craft a series of sermons exploring how Western culture has drifted from God, talking through how we can return to a Judeo-Christian worldview before it's too late.

You're being careful not to get too political in your sermons. You're just trying to invite people to consider how far culture has drifted away from God—which makes it jolting when you start hearing ugly accusations: "Aha! We knew it!" you hear from younger people in your church. "You're preaching Christian Nationalism!"

Does a pastor's concern about a nation's post-Christian trajectory equal "Christian nationalism"?

Such concern might simply mean that a Christian hasn't closed their eyes to future hurt.

Is it possible for us as Christians to engage political issues and still love each other well? Can we have strong convictions about ethics and society—*and* yet hear each other out instead of being lightning quick to label each other as a "wokie" or a "Christian Nationalist"?

A HOPEFUL VISION

We believe it's totally possible to learn into the issues and yet love well. That both-and vision

> **LEAN INTO THE ISSUES AND YET LOVE WELL.**

is the reason for this book. Both of us (John and Daniel) have been traveling this path for a while now. We keep up with current events and cultural trajectories. We have political convictions informed by biblical theology. Yet we remain insistent upon treating people with respect and not letting political debates trip up the way to Jesus.

Yet this vision is harder to see lately. Aaron Renn's article, "The Three Worlds of Evangelicalism,"[1] helpfully describes three stages in the story of the United States' increasing secularization, with less and less room being given to Christian values in the public square. In the article, Renn writes that first, there was the "positive world" (pre-1994) in which society held a largely positive view of Christianity. Then came the "neutral world" (1994-2014) in which Christianity was neither privileged nor out of favor.

We now live in the "negative world" (2014-present) in which society largely has an unfavorable view of Christianity. As Renn describes, evangelical Christians are now split on whether to stay optimistic about their ability to winsomely engage culture (an optimism developed in the "neutral world") or to acknowledge their disfavored status and adjust to the new "negative world."

Now in the "negative world," can we hold fast to a both-and way of engaging deeply while loving widely—and yet loosen our grip

---

[1] Aaron M. Renn, "The Three Worlds of Evangelicalism," *First Things*, February, 2022, https://www.firstthings.com/article/2022/02/the-three-worlds-of-evangelicalism.

on the optimism that this is the way to make people applaud us? Given the volatility of our cultural moment, this vision of being perceptive *and* peaceable might well be the most vilified option by people inside or outside the church.

A storm's coming. Wait—a storm's here. We believe though that this vision remains worth it.

JESUS, BUDDHA, AND THE STORM

A disciple of another guru once approached the Buddha. He boasted to the Buddha of his teacher's ability to remain calm amid thunderous clamor. Once, the disciple described, his teacher was meditating when a procession of five hundred carts passed the teacher by, covering his robe with dust. Somehow, the teacher had remained in his meditative state so deeply that he was genuinely unaware of the procession and had to be told about it after he was done meditating. Could the Buddha claim any such accomplishment?

The Buddha went on to tell the disciple of a time he was meditating in a barn when a storm raged outside. The storm became so severe that lightning struck and killed two farmers and four oxen, just outside the barn. When the Buddha finished meditating and left the barn, he saw a crowd gathered around the corpses and sincerely did not know what had happened. Upon hearing this, the disciple realized that the Buddha was even better at remaining unruffled than his teacher, and the disciple immediately took refuge in the Buddha.[2]

How do Jesus' abilities stack up against those spiritual teachers?

---

[2] "Maha-Parinibbana Sutta: Last Days of the Buddha (DN 16)," translated from the Pali by Sister Vajira and Francis Story, *Access to Insight*, 1998, https://www.accesstoinsight.org/tipitaka/dn/dn.16.1-6.vaji.html

Here is one example. Serious storms can arise without warning on the Sea of Galilee. This happened once when Jesus and his disciples were sailing across the sea. At first, Jesus, similar to the Buddha, was blissfully unaware of the "furious squall" (Mark 4:37). Why? He was asleep on a cushion in the boat's stern. When the boat took on water and began to sink, his disciples panicked and woke Jesus up. "Teacher!" they asked. "Don't you care if we drown?"

Mark 4:39 says, "He got up, rebuked the wind, and said to the waves, 'Quiet! Be still!' Then the wind died down and it was completely calm."

Jesus had the ability to stay untroubled by the storm. But his abilities went beyond that.

When political storms menace the horizon, remember that Jesus' peace "which transcends all understanding" (Philippians 4:7) doesn't transcend our storms in unengaged aloofness. Instead, Jesus' most impressive calm is the result of *engaging* the storm, not shutting it out of mind. As we set out exploring answers through this book on how Christians ought to relate to political tempests, let's not settle for naïve nonchalance or trigger-happy tribalism.

Let's face storms on the horizon the way Jesus showed us. Fully awake, yet filled with peace.

FULLY AWAKE, YET FILLED WITH PEACE.

HOW TO READ THIS BOOK

History teaches us that defective politics can lead to senseless wars, avoidable mass starvations, entrenched corruption, collapsed economies, heartless persecutions, and on and on. Destructive politics mean people with a better vision need to be aware and engaged in their corner of the world. To that end, this book walks you through 21 questions that will help guide you into a political engagement which is both perceptive and peaceable. Each chapter will exercise your intellect and end with a section which will encourage action. We (John and Daniel) are writing from within an American context, and though the United States provides our own political backdrop, we believe you will find the transcultural biblical principles we teach applicable in multiple types of political contexts.

We are so grateful that you are letting us walk with you through these crucial questions, in the hope that we all may grow better at engaging the storms of society as perceptive and peaceable disciples of Jesus.

PART 1 – QUESTIONS ABOUT IDENTITY & PURPOSE

1
WHAT IS THE PURPOSE OF GOVERNMENT?

The Bible is a bit conflicted about human government.

In an ideal world, God would be king, and his will would be done on earth as it is in heaven. Humans would live in loyal partnership with him and serve a viceroys of his rule, extending his aims and agendas on earth. That was the plan when God created the world and human beings.[3]

The problem? We don't live in an ideal world.

We live after the fall in Genesis 3 and outside of Eden. So now it's fair to say that most people don't submit to God's kingship. Many who claim to, actually do not. And even those who do, do so incompletely and imperfectly.

This is where government comes in.

Being under authority is essential to human nature. We were created to operate under God's authority. A common lesson

> **BEING UNDER AUTHORITY IS ESSENTIAL TO HUMAN NATURE.**

---

[3] And this is where the story of the world and human beings is heading. According to the Bible, God is working to restore the earth and human beings to this very thing.

I (John) wanted to communicate when my kids were growing up was, "You will always be under someone's authority. It's the way we're made to operate and it's actually good for you." But fallen humans are self-willed and rebellious. Therefore, human government is necessary to manage and mitigate the chaos that ensues when humans are left to their own devices.

The Bible acknowledges that human government is necessary and is from God (Romans 13:1). It also admits that government tends toward self-enlargement and overreach, and that tendency is often a contributor to and leading cause of injustice.

For example, when Israel insisted on having a king like all the other nations, God consented to their demand but warned them that having a king meant he would conscript their sons for war, enlist them in working in his fields, demand their daughters to serve in his kitchen, seize their property and crops, and tax their income.

The Old Testament prophets regularly call Israel, Judah, and even the surrounding nations—especially their kings and rulers—to account for their injustices. They built palatial estates at the expense of the poor. They took bribes in court and rendered unjust verdicts. They warred and pillaged, with all the horrors commonly associated with those actions, and took people into exile.

Clearly, human government isn't all its supposed to be.

But the answer the Bible gives to this problem is not to be rid of government. The answer it gives is that there must be a just government. What's needed are kings and rulers who uphold righteousness and do justice. Upholding righteousness and doing justice call attention to the main task, the central purpose, that the government is supposed to be about.

An important passage for understanding the role and purpose of the government is Romans 13:1–7. Here, Paul disciples the early Christians and us on how God wants us to think about and relate to the government.

The first thing that Paul points out in this passage has to do with our basic posture toward the government. That posture, according to Paul and the rest of the New Testament, is submission. In a later chapter, we'll discuss when it is appropriate not to submit. But for now, it's important to note that submission in the norm; non-submission is the exception.

Paul also explains why we ought to submit: because governing authority is from God. Paul teaches us that human authorities exist to be *servants* of God.[4] Paul emphasizes this by repeating the word three times. He goes so far as contending that opposing authority is opposing the ordinance of God.

Then Paul goes on to communicate the central purpose of those authorities. As servants of God, rulers, governors, emperors, presidents, prime ministers, and all those who operate on their behalf have a very specific task: to praise good behavior and punish evil behavior (Romans 13:3–4). This is the essential purpose of human

> **GOVERNMENTS PRAISE GOOD BEHAVIOR AND PUNISH EVIL BEHAVIOR.**

government. He even describes the government as an avenger on those who practice evil. Paul also teaches us that it's right to pay taxes in order to support the government in this basic task.

The apostle Peter agrees, putting it very succinctly. The main job of those in authority is "the punishment of evildoers and the praise

---

[4] The word is *diakonos*, the same word for deacons or servants of the church in 1 Timothy 3.

of those who do right" (1 Peter 2:14, NASB). In other words, the Bible views the purpose of human government as expressly limited.

However, there are three problems.

One, as seen in the warning to Israel in the days of Samuel, human government tends toward self-serving expansion. It can keep putting its hands into more areas of life, grabbing more and more tasks, requiring more and more resources, until it begins to snowball out of control.

Two, the world is not an ideal place and most humans, including those in authority, do not submit to God's kingship. So, God's definitions of righteousness and justice often go unheeded or are convoluted. Praising right and punishing wrong are very hard to do when you no longer know what right and wrong are.

Three, because the world is now a less-than-ideal place, humans themselves are a bit of a muddled mix of good and bad. And that means that the people in government are neither all bad nor all good. So, we can't simply identify the "good guys" and the "bad guys" with easy political labels.

Nevertheless, keeping our eyes on the central purpose that God has appointed government to do—praising right and punishing evil—helps us filter out the spin and noise, amid the difficulties, challenges, and ambiguities involved. Keeping this purpose in mind brings a lot of clarity to what we should expect the government to do and to call it to account when it's not doing that in specific ways.

One last thing on this topic: as disciples of Jesus, we must be sure to accept God's definitions of right and wrong. We must saturate ourselves with his word and listen to his commands. When it comes to politics, it's easy to get caught up in rhetoric, be driven by our emotions, or go along with the crowd. We must resist those impulses and heed what God says is righteous and just.

A disciple of Jesus is grateful for the government's role in encouraging good and punishing evil.

ACTION STEPS

1. Read Romans 13:1–7. What do you learn about the purpose of human government and your relationship to it?

2. Based on this passage and other Bible passages you have read, write a short (we're thinking a paragraph) "personal philosophy of government" that will help you filter out the noise and stay focused on the main things to look for in candidates and expect from the government.

2
WHAT DOES OUR FAITH TEACH
THAT OUR SOCIETY NEEDS?

Christianity emerged in a world vastly different from the values espoused by followers of Christ. Slavery was assumed to be a necessary part of a functioning society, and slaves could be thought of as living property and tools.[5] An adulterous wife was a disgrace to be dealt with harshly, but men were free (even expected!) to have numerous sexual partners. Unwanted infants were routinely abandoned, left in the wild to die. Care for the poor, weak, and marginalized was laughable to society at large, contrary to all good sense. And a god who would sacrifice himself for others by dying the most shameful death of all could be pictured as a jackass on a cross![6]

But as Christianity spread, the values of Christ—values currently being taken for granted as good and right—transformed the Roman Empire and the world.

> **THE VALUES OF CHRIST TRANSFORMED THE ROMAN EMPIRE.**

---

[5] Aristotle, *Politics*, 1.1253b.
https://www.perseus.tufts.edu/hopper/text?doc=Perseus%3Atext%3A1999.01.0058%3Abook%3D1%3Asection%3D1253b
[6] See the "Alexamenos Graffito" found in Rome.

To be fair, the Church has not always lived up to the values she espouses. Nevertheless, over the course of history, the values of the Christian faith have brought great good to the world and our society needs Christians to bring these values into the world today.

In this chapter, we want to highlight a few of these values, and we do so for two reasons. One, these values ought to guide us at the ballot box, shaping the kind of people and policies we vote for. And two, these values must guide how we conduct ourselves in conversation and on social media as we engage with the political process. It's far more important that we honor Jesus by embodying these values than that we "win" an election.

Here are a few of these key values.

- **Truth** – The Christian faith teaches that there is truth about the world, including moral truth. Truth can be known, and it's rooted in who God is and what humans are. This truth provides guidelines and guardrails for human flourishing, so that to reject it leads to great harm to our wellbeing. Our society desperately needs to know that there is truth for their life. Not angry truth. Not arrogant truth. But they need the idea that there is real truth rooted in the way things really are. Truth that is in sync with the way life, the world, and humans are designed to operate, so that as we acquire it, individually and collectively we begin to function the way we are meant to function. In the absence of such truth, all that remains to govern society are power and feelings.
- **Human worth and dignity** – Rooted in the creation account in Genesis is the conviction that all people are made in the

image of God. Thus, all people have worth and dignity. This has led Christians to do acts such as rescue abandoned infants, risk their lives to care for those sick with the plague, start hospitals, provide homes for orphans, help the infirm and disabled, contend for the abolition of slavery, argue that all people are created equal, and fight for human rights.

• **Care for the poor, lowly, and marginalized** – Because Christ himself modeled it and because all people have dignity and worth, Christians care for the less fortunate. They have fed the hungry, welcomed the outcasts, elevated the status of women and children, provided education for those with no access to it, and sought to help the powerless.

• **Marriage and sexuality** – The historic Christian vision for marriage and sexuality has protected women and taught men to practice loyal, covenant love. It elevated the value of children and provided a secure environment for children to be nurtured in. Indeed, if everyone practiced the historic Christian vision for marriage and sexuality, there would be no rape, no sexual harassment, no divorces due to infidelity, no pedophilia, and no pornography. Sex trafficking, along with a great many other societal evils connected to sex, would be eliminated.

• **Generosity** – According to Non-Profit Source, Americans give over 450 billion dollars to charity annually.[7] Deep in our cultural consciousness lies the notion that giving to meet the needs of others is good. This idea stems from the influence of Christianity. Generosity is one of the core values of the

---

[7] "The Ultimate List of Charitable Giving Statistics of 2023," *Non-Profit Source*, https://nonprofitssource.com/online-giving-statistics/.

Christian faith, motivated by and patterned after what God has done for us in Christ.

• **Justice** – Another great good that the Christian faith brings into the world is the conviction that all people ought to be treated fairly and rightly. There should be no double standards—one for those with money and power and another for those without. The law must be applied fairly and equitably to all people.

> **THE LAW MUST BE APPLIED FAIRLY.**

• **Forgiveness** – One of the most distinctive practices of Christianity is that of forgiveness when wronged. Jesus taught us to forgive no matter how many times we've been wronged and modeled it on the cross by asking God to forgive those who killed him. What's more, by offering himself, he forgave each one of us as well. Therefore, we are to love our enemies and forgive whoever wrongs us.

• **Hope** – Hope is in short supply among many in our society. Christianity promises a glorious future that is good for the earth and for human beings. It offers meaning to our lives, a purpose to our sufferings, and a motivation for right living.

• **Love** – Core to these values is the Christian value of self-giving love—the kind of love patterned after Jesus' own self-sacrifice, especially that demonstrated on the cross.

What our society often fails to recognize is that, although culturally we have taken many of these values for granted, such values were foreign to the cultures of the ancient world until Christianity arrived. The early church changed the world through preaching the gospel and teaching people to obey Christ. These teachings transformed the world to such an extent that many of these values, which were once unheard of, are now widely considered good.

Thus, for a very long time, beginning with many of the United States' founding fathers, there was often overlap between the values of the United States and the values of the Kingdom of God. This overlap often beguiled us into thinking we were a "Christian nation." Christians assumed we belonged and that our ideals would always be treated with acceptance and respect. Some even went so far as to contend that with enough lobbyist pressure and with the right candidates in office, the United States could become some sort of Christian utopia.

But the values listed above are not guaranteed American values. They are Kingdom of God values. They are rooted in the teachings of Jesus.

See, here's the thing: distinctively Christian values such as these are based in the beliefs of the Christian worldview. Eliminating the beliefs uproots the values. So, as the beliefs that undergird these values have increasingly been rejected by our culture, the values themselves have begun to recede in our society. Some values once considered *good* are now seen as odd or looked on with suspicion and even hostility. This trend will only continue to happen as long as people by and large reject Christian beliefs. And thus, the church in America now finds itself in territory new to itself, but not new to the church as a whole. In the next chapter, we will explore what the church's status and role are supposed to be in relation to the surrounding culture.

A disciple of Jesus lives out values that help society flourish.

ACTION STEP

1. Read Ephesians 4:17–5:5. Note all the values and virtues that show up there. Also note how they are tied to learning the way of Jesus and his kingdom. Examine yourself: are there ways, especially when it comes to engaging in politics, that you have failed to live out these virtues that you need to confess? How will these virtues shape your political aims and interactions going forward?

3
ARE YOU CLEAR ON WHAT GOD CALLS YOU TO BE?

Here's a question for you: are you an American who happens to be a Christian, or are you a Christian who happens to live in America?

In other words, what is your core identity that shapes your beliefs, values, and practices? Is it being a citizen of the United States (or whatever country you live in)? Or is it your primary allegiance to King Jesus?

As noted in the previous chapter, there was a long period (recall Renn's "positive world" described in the introduction) when some of the values of the United States and the values of Christ's kingdom overlapped in large ways. This meant that direct and explicit challenges to our allegiance to King Jesus were fewer and farther between. That felt safety lulled us into thinking there was less urgency to think through the exact nature of our status as God's people in relation to the society in which we find ourselves. So, when it came to cultural and political engagement, we often hadn't clarified how our deepest allegiance as disciples of Jesus was to play out and what our highest responsibilities were.

But the early church did not have that luxury. As the church moved out into the Greco-Roman world of the first century, it encountered a culture whose beliefs, values, and practices were vastly different from its own. Some of the church's beliefs and values were seen as odd. Some were considered downright treasonous.

How should Christians think of themselves in relation to the communities in which they find themselves? In a number of places, the New Testament answers that question and thus can help us think through who we are and what God calls us to be in relationship to the surrounding culture. Let us highlight a few key themes.

AN OUTPOST OF HEAVEN

Writing to a small church in the Roman colony of Philippi, the apostle Paul says, "But our **OUR CITIZENSHIP IS IN HEAVEN.** citizenship is in heaven. And we eagerly await a Savior from there, the Lord Jesus Christ" (Philippians 3:20).

Paul's words here play off the Philippian civic situation which shaped their entire social identity. About a hundred years before Paul wrote his letter to the Philippian Christians, one of the key battles of the Roman civil war had been fought on the plains outside the city of Philippi. Veterans from the war were settled there, and the city was granted the high honor of being a Roman colony. In fact, it was bestowed the honor of *Ius Italicum*, meaning that even though the city was in Macedonia, it was treated like a little piece of Italy, with all the rights and benefits that went with it.

They lived in Philippi but were citizens of Rome. They paid fewer taxes and had greater Roman rights. They were like a little outpost of Rome there in the homeland of Alexander the Great. And the purpose of such citizenship was to export Roman values and practices throughout the region. That is, the citizens of Rome in Philippi would live out and pass on the culture of Rome.

Just like that, as Paul describes, the Christians are citizens of heaven living in Philippi.

And not only that, but they also wait for a Savior from heaven. The ordinary citizens of Philippi called the emperor savior and lord and looked to Rome for peace and security. But not the Christians. They were to look to heaven. Their Savior was the Lord Jesus the Messiah.

Paul instructs us, therefore, to think of ourselves as citizens of another realm, the kingdom of God in Christ. We are an outpost of heaven wherever we live, representing heaven's King. And the point of that citizenship is not to hunker down and wait until we can go to heaven. No, Paul's point in playing off the Philippian situation is that we're here to embody, display, and champion the culture of heaven in our little corner of earth. This means we embody the values and virtues of heaven in our everyday lives. This means we invite others into the kingdom of heaven by making disciples. We do this all the while waiting for heaven's King to return, knowing that he is the only Savior who can set everything right.

EXILES AND FOREIGNERS

The book of 1 Peter is also very important in helping us think through who we are called to be. Throughout the letter, Peter repeatedly communicates that followers of Jesus are "foreigners" in their own land. There's an out-of-placeness—a cultural misfit-ness—because we are now part of God's kingdom in Christ. Our beliefs and values are now shaped by King Jesus and thus in many ways won't match with the beliefs and values of the city and country we are living in.

Peter uses two key words to express this concept:

- **Sojourner or stranger** – This particular word focuses on staying for a while in an unfamiliar and strange place, a place where you don't fully belong. It reflects the idea of exile.
- **Foreigner** – This word overlaps in meaning with the previous word but emphasizes living in a place where the way of life is contrary to our own. It speaks to being a foreign resident.

The fact that Christians are exiles and foreigners wherever they live means that our beliefs, values, and practices must be shaped more by the kingdom of God than by the culture around us. It reminds us that God's kingdom receives our deepest allegiance and his honor must be our highest concern, far above our national identity.

ROYAL PRIESTHOOD AND HOLY NATION

Peter teaches that we are called to be a royal priesthood and a holy nation (1 Peter 2:9). This language derives from God's description of Israel in Exodus 19. It designates the vocation God intends for his people then and now, and entails certain responsibilities we have on behalf of God in relation to our surrounding society.

First, Christians are a royal priesthood. Priests represent people to God and God to the people. So

> **CHRISTIANS ARE A ROYAL PRIESTHOOD.**

as exiles and foreigners living where we do, we stand between God and the world. We represent God to the world and bring the world to God.

Second, we are also a holy nation. *Holiness* equals *difference.* To be a holy nation, therefore, means we are to be distinct in our way of life. So just as Paul tells the Philippians, we are like a nation within a nation, displaying the culture of God's kingdom to the world around us.

And the goal of being a kingdom of priests and a holy nation is to "proclaim the excellencies of Him who has called you out of darkness into His marvelous light" (1 Peter 2:9, NASB).

How does Peter suggest we do that?

His basic answer is, by displaying a way of life that is excellent (or beautiful; kalos in Greek) and by doing good in the community where you live (see 1 Peter 2:11–12). Peter immediately applies this to three well-known social institutions of his day: submitting to civic authorities, working as a household servant, and marriage. In every context, he points out that displaying a beautiful way of life and doing good are what believers are to do even if the civic authorities are foolish, the master of the house is unjust, or you are married to an unbeliever. This is how we carry out our calling as a kingdom of priests and a holy nation.

THREE IMPLICATIONS

Allow us to draw out three implications for how to live out who we are in our corner of the world:

First, our expectations ought to be marked by a healthy realism. This is a fallen world, and that includes our country. Our Savior doesn't come from Washington. So, though we can pray and work for good policies to replace bad ones, we must not place our hopes in who is in office or in a particular party.

Second, though we live here, our identity is not from here. The values and virtues that drive us at the voting booth must be shaped by and in sync with the culture of God's kingdom.

Third, the manner in which we "wage wars," including political ones, must not be according to the flesh (2 Corinthians 10:3) but in line with the character of Christ (e.g., Galatians 5:22–23; Colossians 3:12–17). In the way we conduct ourselves, therefore, we must display the excellency and beauty of God's kingdom. Our core mission is to be Jesus' ambassadors by making disciples. We must not get so caught up in political culture wars that we drag the name of Jesus through the mud.

A disciple of Jesus lives as a citizen of heaven strategically placed in a particular corner of the world.

ACTION STEPS

1. Read 1 Peter 2:11–3:9 and note some of the areas of life and ways in which Christians are to do good/right in their public life.

2. Let's reflect on two truths we need to hold in tension. One, our citizenship is first and foremost in heaven, so our identity, values, and hope come from there. But, two, defective politics harm people and the world. List a few implications of how this tension ought to affect our political engagement.

4
CAN YOU SPOT EASY GOSPELS?

The French Revolution from 1789–1799 aimed to level everybody to the equal status of "citizen." In so doing, it meant to abolish the aristocracy, state religion, and monarchy. Yet for the first three of those Revolutionary years, King Louis XVI was still the king.

How did Louis manage to stay in the favor of the revolutionaries for that many years into the Revolution? From what historians tell us, he was indecisive and desired very much to be loved by the people, so he went along to get along with the revolutionaries as best as he could. He submitted to the newly formed constitution and became a constitutional monarch.

Meanwhile, the Revolutionaries began wearing a red "liberty cap," which looked like a stocking cap. Soon, the cap was the fashionable thing to wear for anyone wanting to show solidarity with the movement. During public executions within the two years known as the "Reign of Terror," women would sit beside the guillotines and knit liberty caps.

One evening, when Louis was still king at least in name, revolutionaries stormed his palace. One insurgent approached him and held out a liberty cap perched atop a sword. Louis dutifully took the cap, put it on, and the crowd cheered.

The royal crown was replaced by the liberty cap.

It is entirely possible to be part of one kingdom, in theory. Yet all the while, you're actually owned by a political party.

> **THE ROYAL CROWN WAS REPLACED BY THE LIBERTY CAP.**

A READY-MADE RED CAP

In our day, we're being offered a red cap or a blue cap—easy, ready-made, prepackaged versions of the gospels on the political right and left. Those "gospels" take a lot less of digging into what Jesus taught and a lot more of listening to talk shows and checking social media in order to learn what others say Jesus *really* cares about.

This temptation has been going on for a while. Here's a quick story in four parts. When you read this, see if you can figure out whom this story is about.

1. When he came to power, he rescued the church from a season of persecution and began to bless the church with special favors.

2. The church began to look at this man as their protector, even as something of a savior. They had nothing but good to

say about him, and nothing but bad to say about his political enemies.

3. He began to use the church as a way of unifying his realm, and so when he saw disunity within the church, he brought the church together to resolve the issue and reunify.

4. When this man died and his son came to power, the son used his influence within the church to try to force the church to adopt beliefs that were not based in the Bible.

Which person are we talking about? It's the Roman Emperor Constantine. He came to power in the year A.D. 306, ended the persecution against the church, and converted to Christianity himself. The church responded by showering him with praise as their protector. The church denounced his political enemies as being the enemies of God.

Constantine used the church to bring unity into his empire, which had been divided into Eastern and Western halves. When Emperor Constantine died and his son Constantius became emperor, Constantius saw in Arianism, a heretical version of Christianity, what he believed would be an even more efficient way to unify the empire. Because Arianism taught that Jesus wasn't quite God, this version was easier for pagans to accept than orthodox Christianity. Thus, Constantius tried to force the bishops in his empire to accept Arianism.

When you think about the ready-made red cap being presented to the American church, you might consider the story of Constantine. The red-cap version of the gospel is a gospel framed by conservative, red-state concerns. According to this version of the gospel, what *really* matters to true followers of Jesus are the items listed in a conservative, red-state political platform: free-market capitalism, fiscal conservativism, gun rights, etc. The idea according to this version is that to be a faithful Christian, a person needs to be discipled into rightist politics. They need red-state political voices to teach them what's worth fretting about and fighting for as a Christian.

When it comes to the red cap being offered to the church—as a ready-made, prepackaged version of the gospel—it's got the vibes of the story of Constantine all over again:

1. Rightist politicians can be quick to offer to rescue churches from persecution by giving them religious freedom and blessing churches with special favor.

2. Churches can begin to look at rightist politicians as their protectors, even as something analogous to saviors. If our churches choose the red cap, we can find ourselves having nothing but good to say about our favorite rightist politicians and nothing but bad to say about leftist politicians.

3. Rightist politicians can begin to use the church as a way of unifying their constituencies and giving spiritual validity to their platforms.

4. When they have established their influence within churches, just like Constantius, they can try to force the church to adopt beliefs that are not based in the Bible.

Thus, we can end up taking our cues more from political talk shows than from the New Testament, and we can end up becoming one hand clapping. We can end up feeling nothing but contempt for the other side of the aisle, because we believe that on *this* side, we're right. On this side, we have morals. We can end up believing that, if only our side could win back power, then we've finally got hope.

Leaning to the right in one's politics isn't the problem. The problem lies in wearing the red cap and embracing its easy, ready-made version of the gospel—which is not how the gospel works.

> # LEANING TO THE RIGHT IN ONE'S POLITICS ISN'T THE PROBLEM.

Some Christians have grown up in churches that emanate self-righteousness: "*We're* right about basically everything. *We* have the right beliefs. *We* have the right views. *We're* good. We care about family values and moral absolutes. We don't do sexual deviance. We don't do abortion. We don't believe Marxism and paganism and feminism and all the isms. *We're* right. *We're* good. God smiles down on *us.*"

Some Christians, having grown up in that kind of religiosity, have concluded about the church, "You say you care about Jesus and about reaching lost people. You really just care about *yourself.* Yours is a gospel of JUST US." So they decide to leave that version of Christianity behind. "You may be all about JUST US. We're going to be all about JUSTICE."[8]

And as they're making that transition, guess who meets them with a welcoming smile? It's someone offering them a *blue* cap. We'll learn more about the blue cap in the next chapter.

In the meantime, please remember this: if you are going to engage politically in a way that is perceptive and peaceable, you must

---

[8] We first heard the expression "just us" (as opposed to "justice") from sociologist Os Guinness.

be able to spot—and resist—easy, prepackaged, and false versions of the gospel.

A disciple of Jesus resists easy, prepackaged versions of gospel.

ACTION STEPS

1. Read Matthew 23:13–28. There is a sense in which the Pharisees often resembled "red cap people." They felt secure in their own ethical righteousness. They felt they knew what God expected. And their aim was to be as right and holy as possible so that God would bless their nation. What are some things that stand out to you from Jesus' critique of the Pharisees here?

2. The problem is not leaning rightist in one's politics. The problem is accepting the "red cap" and embracing its easy, ready-made version of the gospel. Make a list of some of the main dangers you see of believing a red-cap version of the gospel.

5
DO YOU KNOW THE TIMES YOU'RE LIVING IN?

One of the most memorable songs in the movie *Three Amigos!* is sung by a "singing bush." The song is called "Blow the Man Down." The song is so random it's easy to assume it was made for the movie. Yet "Blow the Man Down" is actually a sea shanty at least as old as the 1860s. It's also not a bad caption for the current cultural moment.

Os Guinness's *The Dust of Death* is a 1973 assessment of the 1960s counterculture. In this book, Guinness describes the secular West's onetime "belief in the self-sufficiency of man," and how, "Twentieth-century upheavals have cruelly blown this apart."[9] If it was once a compliment to be known as "the man," the 60s counterculture made "the Man" into a self-absorbed, greedy person in power to oppose and resist. The counterculture worked to bring down the "System"—meaning the political, economic, and social powers of the day.[10] Antiwar protests, Marxist radicalism, and psychedelic escapism were all ways meant to "blow the Man down."

---

[9] Os Guinness, *Dust of Death: A Critique of the Establishment and the Counter Culture—and a Proposal for a Third Way* (Downers Grove: InterVarsity Christian Fellowship, 1973), 16, 19.
[10] Guinness, *Dust of Death*, 118.

Yet the Man persists into the 21st century, and so does the countercultural impulse to root him out and bring him down. This impulse has only strengthened and entrenched itself in the most powerful institutions of the Western world.

Do you want to understand the times you live in? Then you need to understand this impulse and its influence.

A READY-MADE BLUE CAP

In the previous chapter, we learned about a rightist ready-made version of the gospel. There's a leftist ready-made version of the gospel, too. And as Christians put on the

> **THERE'S A LEFTIST READY-MADE VERSION OF THE GOSPEL, TOO.**

blue cap, they may not know it yet, but a whole lot more is about to change than just their political views.

In the modern Western world, we in the church are being conditioned to move from a worldview centered on God and what he says in the Bible to a worldview centered on oppressed people. It's a worldview in which what's true and good and just are rooted not in the teachings of Scripture, but in the lived experienced of oppressed people.

The blue cap system is often called "progressivism." Different versions and facets of progressivism go by different names, and in particular we're going to dial in to a version of progressivism called "intersectional feminism." (Even if you are not familiar with the term "intersectional feminism," you'll likely recognize its tenets when we begin describing it.)

A disclaimer: We are not saying that there are no insights to be learned from intersectional feminism. There are insights we can learn from listening to intersectional feminists as with any worldview. But we are going to be describing intersectional feminism as an ethical system, and as an ethical system, it directly challenges many of the claims of historic Christianity. We believe that if one wants to understand the modern Western world, one needs to understand intersectional feminism.

Intersectional feminism starts by emphasizing that certain groups have privilege and power. Accordingly, people who are white, heterosexual, cisgender, male, and Christian have enjoyed unearned privilege in Western culture. Society has been structured to prioritize these groups' interests and marginalize the interests of non-privileged people. As a result, these privileged groups enjoy power over others, and their decisions are motivated by maintaining that power, even when cloaked in the guise of "I'm just trying to teach biblical truth."

On the other hand, there are groups who live at the "intersections" of oppression. There are people who are racial *and* religious minorities (so, for example, a Latino Wiccan). There are people who are gender *and* sexual orientation minorities (for example, a bisexual woman). These people living at the intersections have been victimized by privileged people in power. When someone's identity is rooted at these intersections, they have a unique perspective on justice and truth which privileged people are unable to understand as fully.

So, when does intersectional feminism go from describing power dynamics to challenging claims of Christianity? According to intersectional feminism, any group with unearned power and privilege in Western civilization is to be viewed with suspicion. And since Christianity helped build Western civilization, intersectional feminism conditions people to view Christianity with a mood of deep cynicism. Christian claims of what's true/false or right/wrong are meant to maintain Christian power and marginalize the opposition. And when Christians are told they're privileged and obsessed with power, if they overreact and get angry, it just reinforces the narrative: they're all about maintaining power.

So, how do intersectional feminists decide what is true and false? Right and wrong? Just and unjust? It's all grounded in the lived experience of oppressed people.

IT'S ALL GROUNDED IN THE LIVED EXPERIENCE OF OPPRESSED PEOPLE.

Let's say, for example, I'm a Christian and I start to embrace intersectional feminism. Does anything change? Quite a bit, in fact. If I'm an intersectional feminist, eventually I've got to stop caring so much about what the Bible says concerning what it means to be male or female, and I've got to start asking what oppressed people, transgender people in particular, say it means to be male or female. I've got to stop focusing on what the Bible teaches about marriage and sexuality, and I've got to ask what oppressed people, in particular homosexuals and bisexuals, say about marriage and sexuality. I've got to stop caring so much about what the Bible says concerning forgiveness, and I've got to ask what oppressed people say about who should and should not be forgiven.

This ready-made version of the gospel is about taking claims regarding what's true and good out of the hands of the God of the

Bible and rooting our beliefs of truth and ethics in the lived experiences of oppressed people.

The more people around you who begin thinking like intersectional feminists, the more pressure you will face to change many of your Christian beliefs, or at least to go quiet about them. If you're a church leader, the more people in your church who embrace intersectional feminism, the more pressure you will feel to soften your church's tone about Christian beliefs and eventually change those beliefs altogether. As Bryan Laughlin and Doug Ponder describe it, the trajectory when it comes to changing our views about difficult doctrines is first, silence, then complexification, and then capitulation.[11] If you've been successfully pressured into silence about your biblical views about, say, sexual ethics, then you're likely on your way.

MULTIPLE OFFERS

So, in summary of these last two chapters, how do you navigate politics without losing the gospel? Realize that you're being offered a red cap and its easy, ready-made, prepackaged version of the gospel. *And* you're being offered a blue cap with its easy, ready-made version of the gospel.

There's the gospel of JUST US. *We're* right. *We're* good. God loves us.

---

[11] Bryan Laughlin and Doug Ponder, "Christianity and Functional Liberalism (or How Evangelicalism Denies the Faith)," *Sola Ecclesia*, November 8, 2023, https://solaecclesia.org/articles/christianity-and-functional-liberalism/.

There's the gospel of JUSTICE—so that all the people that Christians have supposedly shoved to the side are now brought to the center and handed the gavel.

And then there's the gospel of JESUS.

A disciple of Jesus understands the times and refuses to let the gospel be coopted by them.

ACTION STEPS

1. Read John 19:12–15 and reflect on this: what are some ways that leaders who say they trust God can end up putting their faith in "Caesar"?

2. Identify 3–4 indicators in your own heart and life that suggest you are beginning to put to your trust in the government and/or politics.

6
IN WHAT WAYS HAS THE CHURCH INTERACTED WITH THE STATE THROUGHOUT HISTORY?

First, some bad news. The bad news is that, historically, churches haven't always resisted the allure of false, prepackaged gospels. Sometimes churches have traded their call to be the people of God for the prospect of being a branch of the government. In this way, they give the government a stamp of spiritual legitimacy, but in the process they lose their voice of truth and prophetic critique.

The good news is that there have been other, more biblical, ways that churches have interacted with governments throughout history. Before we briefly describe four models of church-state interaction, it will be helpful to quickly review the story of church history.

The church has had over 2,000 years of history, and it can be difficult to keep the highlights clear in one's mind. One way to help people remember some of the major events of church history (with an emphasis on the church in the Western world) is to use game board pieces:

1. Thimble: The Monopoly thimble represents the early church up against Roman persecution—think sharp metal objects like needles—and yet standing strong under the opposition.

2. King: The chess king represents the church under Emperor Constantine, who ended the persecution against the church and gave it special privileges.

3. Iron: The Monopoly iron is for when the church brought together its leaders to iron out some core theology through church councils.

4. Knight: The chess knight symbolizes the invasion of barbarians (e.g., picture the Huns on horseback) which brought down the Western half of the empire and initiated the Dark Ages.

5. Bishop: The chess bishop is the pope, the bishop of the church in Rome, who stepped up to lead during the chaos of the Dark Ages. Although the Roman bishop was already perceived as one of the premier leaders of the church, these years grew the bishop's leadership over the church as a whole.

6. Checker: The checker is the "Holy Roman Empire," initiated when the pope crowned Charlemagne as emperor ("King me.").

7. Rook: The chess rook, which can only go two directions, represents the two directions the church split in A.D. 1054, when West (Roman Catholic) and East (Eastern Orthodox) finally separated in the "Great Schism."

8. Top Hat: The Monopoly top hat stands for the growing prominence, pride, and pragmatism of the Roman Catholic church hierarchy.

9. Pawn: The chess pawn symbolizes the Protestant Reformation which ordained the common Christian as a priest (the "priesthood of all believers").

10. Ship: The Monopoly ship stands for the discoveries of the New World, a world which Catholic and Protestant missionaries would largely convert.

11. Dice: Dice symbolize the emergence of new philosophies of chance, like Darwinism, which cast doubt on there being a divine purpose behind everything.

12. Shoe: Finally, the Monopoly shoe stands for the church, which continues to march on.

The problem with the simplicity of these twelve steps is that numbers 6–9 in this list actually happen twice. The first time, pope crowns emperor (checker), church splits in two (rook), pope enjoys prestige (top hat), and Reformation champions common man (pawn). The second time follows on the heels of the first, rushing through them more quickly. The Protestant Reformers soon began "kinging" their own alliances with princes and city councils (checker). Meanwhile, the Protestants split into their own divisions (rook). For example, Martin Luther allied with German princes, John Calvin was invited to bring reform to the city of Geneva, Switzerland, as was Ulrich Zwingli for Zurich, Switzerland. Such civic alliances invited new Protestant prestige (top hat).

Not surprisingly, the new powers made for new pawns. Protestants proudly remember the

> ## THE NEW POWERS MADE FOR NEW PAWNS.

German Diet of Speyer in 1529 as when Protestant princes boldly stood up to the Holy Roman Emperor and successfully protested the religious persecution against them. That is the Diet from which the movement derived its name "Protestant." Yet it is also the Diet at which both Catholic powers and new Protestant powers joined together against a new band of pawns, a group called the Anabaptists.[12]

The Reformation had successfully fortified itself with political alliances, as had the church under Constantine, and, yet again, a formerly persecuted minority all too quickly forgot what it had felt like to be persecuted. Lutherans, Calvinists, and Zwinglians removed their "pawn" labels and hung them around the necks of the Anabaptists.

Who were the Anabaptists? The Anabaptists insisted on baptizing only those who were old enough to make that decision themselves. They were convinced that to join the church should be a choice, and a weighty one at that. So, in 1524, when the Conrad Grebel family was blessed with a baby boy, they had a somber decision to make. Should they follow the custom of their Swiss town, Zurich, and baptize their infant? Seeing infant baptism nowhere in Scripture, the Grebels refused, their stance emboldening other families to do the same.

Then came 1525. On January 17, the Zurich city council decreed that all families with unbaptized children would baptize them within the week or be banished from Zurich. Four days later, the night

---

[12] George Huntston Williams, *The Radical Reformation*, 3rd ed. (Philadelphia: Truman State University Press, 1992), 358–359.

of January 21, these families made their decision at Felix Manz's house, where they decided it was time to sever themselves from the church of their city council.[13] Though sprinkled as infants, they walked to the city square under nightfall and baptized each other in the city square's fountain. The Anabaptists went on to struggle to survive the brutal persecution they went on to face in both Protestant and Catholic lands. However, many of their beliefs, including their repudiation of church-state alliance, survive today (most noticeably in Mennonite, Amish, and Hutterite communities).

Against this church history backdrop, we can make better sense of the various kinds of church-state interaction we see throughout church history. We list them here, in order from greater to less church-state interaction. As you'll notice, each level of interaction fits well with the reception given to the church at the time. Far more can be said about these models (we encourage you to check out the classic book, *Christ and Culture*, for a more in-depth description), but this will at least give some snapshots of how churches have interacted with the state:[14]

- **(S) Synthesis** – An S has two semi-circles that look like each other and blend into each other. What we're calling S-level interaction is close interaction between church and state, such that there is a synthesis of sorts between the two. Especially in its medieval years, the Roman Catholic Church experienced a synthesis of church and state. During these years, church and

---

[13] Bruce L. Shelley, *Church History in Plain Language*, 2nd ed. (Nashville: Thomas Nelson Publishers, 1995), 250.
[14] In addition to Reinhold Niebuhr's *Christ and Culture*, you can find a popular-level explanation in a sermon preached by David Young at North Boulevard Church of Christ on July 23, 2023. See David Young, "Church and State 2," July 23, 2023 https://northboulevard.com/sermon/church-and-state-2.

state were closely allied while each carried out an important, distinct role for society. This view was articulated by Catholic theologian Thomas Aquinas.

• **(C) Conversion** – The letter C helps us picture a change, a transformation. The shape of C suggests a turn ahead. Thus, the C stands for "conversion." John Calvin taught that the state is a gift from God and that the church can help convert/transform it so that what is corrupted can be made godlier and more just. Abraham Kuyper, Calvinist and onetime Prime Minister of the Netherlands, famously said, "There is not a square inch in the whole domain of our human existence over which Christ, who is Sovereign over all, does not cry, Mine!"[15] Thus, the church can and should seek to transform all layers of society on behalf of Christ.

• **(T) Tension** – In a T, you see two sides divided by a solid line. In a T, both sides kind of do their own thing, and there's not a lot of interaction between them. A T-model church-state interaction is going to stand for the word "tension." Martin Luther taught that there is a necessary, ongoing tension between the church and the state. God has given one set of ethics to the church (with priority given to grace) and another to the state (with priority given to justice). It is permissible for Christians to be involved in government, but the distinction between the two needs to be kept clear.

• **(O) Opposition** – Notice how an O is sealed off from the outside. It suggests a strict separation between what's inside and outside. In this way, Anabaptists emphasized a sharp,

---

[15] James D. Bratt, Ed, *Abraham Kuyper: A Centennial Reader* (Grand Rapids: William B. Eerdmans Publishing Company, 1998), 461.

impassable division between the values of the church and the state. It is better for the church and its members not to get involved in governmental affairs (e.g., military service, state jobs, etc.); even voting may be discouraged.

In chapter 1, we looked at what the Bible teaches about the government and its purpose. Its primary purpose is praising right and punishing wrong (see Romans

> **THE GOVERNMENT'S PRIMARY PURPOSE IS PRAISING RIGHT AND PUNISHING WRONG.**

13:1–7; 1 Peter 2:14). Keeping that purpose in mind, which model do you find the most legitimate way of church-state interaction? Are each of them valid depending on how much the church is invited to participate? At what points do the opportunities become temptations?

We want to suggest that, wherever you land when it comes to these models, it's worth noting that, the closer a church gets to an S-model of interaction, the more temptation there will be for trying to let politics do the heavy lifting of expanding Christ's kingdom (which is not how his kingdom expands). At the same time, the closer a church gets to an O-model of interaction, the greater the temptation to circle the wagons and not permeate society with the kinds of values our faith provides and which society needs (see chapter 2).

A disciple of Jesus is in the world (not trying to escape it) but not of the world (not absorbing its selfish ambitions).

ACTION STEPS

1. Peter reminds us that we are foreigners and exiles. Read 1 Peter 1:1–2 and 2:11–12 and reflect on how Peter wants Christians to think about their status as foreigners and exiles where they live. What are some implications of that? How does that status influence our political aims and involvement?

2. Which of the four models shared at the end of this chapter have you tended toward and why? What, if any, value do you see in the other three models?

7
WHAT HILLS ARE WORTH DYING ON?

Looking back, one of the great disappointments of 2020 was seeing Christians choosing the wrong "hills" on which to die. Friendships severed and churches split over foolish reasons. "Can you believe that some churches have split over the color of the carpet?" *Crazy,* we think. And yet some of our richly-resourced, multi-staffed churches of 2020 threatened to tear apart over what to do with even thinner strips of cloth—called masks.

We are not as strong as we think we are.

Many churches need to go back to school for a great many lessons. Our 2020 grade card showed us barely passing in some core classes, such as prayer and fasting, compassion, and disciple making.

In addition to these, however, there's a new class we ought to consider enrolling in as quickly as possible: *Hills to Die On 101.*

We need a Masterclass taught by Jesus. At least two of the lectures would be called "Hills to Die On" and "Hills to Withdraw From." These would deal with being able to tell the difference between a good hill to die on and a bad one. In John 6, we read about Jesus withdrawing from a hill that was presented to him by a zealous mob:

"After the people saw the sign Jesus performed, they began to say, 'Surely this is the Prophet who is to come into the world.' Jesus, knowing that they intended to come and make him king by force, withdrew again to a mountain by himself." (John 6:14–15)

JESUS WITHDREW AGAIN TO A MOUNTAIN BY HIMSELF.

Jesus passed up mediocre hills so he could set his focus on the one which would accomplish the most for the world. As his final Passover approached, Jesus recognized the hill he'd been called to:

"The hour has come for the Son of Man to be glorified. Very truly I tell you, unless a kernel of wheat falls to the ground and dies, it remains only a single seed. But if it dies, it produces many seeds. Anyone who loves their life will lose it, while anyone who hates their life in this world will keep it for eternal life." (John 12:23–25)

After the 2020 presidential election in the United States, as Joe Biden's electoral dominance over Donald Trump showed no signs of giving way, a prominent evangelical leader urged his followers to make reversing the results the hill to die on: "We need to fight to the death, to the last drop of blood, because it's worth it."[16] That's a hill for us to die on? *Capitol* Hill?

[16] Rod Dreher, "Eric Metaxas's American Apocalypse," *The American Conservative*, December 10, 2020, https://www.theamericanconservative.com/eric-metaxas-trump-bloodshed-american-apocalypse-live-not-by-lies/.

The apostle Peter was insistent that Jesus' followers choose our hill of martyrdom wisely.

"If you suffer, it should not be as a murderer or thief or any other kind of criminal, or even as a meddler. However, if you suffer as a Christian, do not be ashamed, but praise God that you bear that name." (1 Peter 4:15–16)

Dear friends, please choose your hill wisely.

A violently divided nation is frightening. And so is one in which there is no room for dissent, such as a totalitarian North Korea. It is *unity in diversity* that is beautiful. Unity in diversity is even suggested in our nation's singular-plural name: the United States.

Similarly, we shouldn't aim for complete political and cultural uniformity in our churches. The unity we are to have is to be grace-based, a unity amid political and cultural diversity. If we can figure out how to love each other well amid cultural tensions and political disagreements, then we can show a wounded nation the way forward.

If there are political differences within your church, then *praise God!* That means that your church has not circled-the-wagons so tightly that outsiders won't ever feel welcome. Differences also mean that you have a great starting point for living out the biblical commands to "seek peace and pursue it" (1 Peter 3:11) and to "make every effort to keep the unity of the Spirit through the bond of peace" (Ephesians 4:3). We cannot seek peace with people who blandly agree in every detail as if the gathering were a political cult rather than a church.

Do not make the eradication of political differences within your church your hill. Instead, use those political differences as the opportunity to clarify and unify around the convictions that matter most to Jesus, and grow stronger as a result.

What are the convictions that matter most to Jesus? A helpful way to discern hills worth dying on is to think in terms of essential, important, and personal elements.

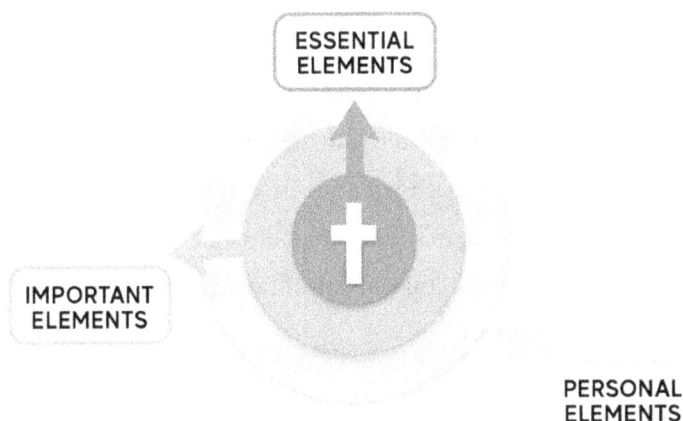

ESSENTIAL
ELEMENTS

IMPORTANT
ELEMENTS

PERSONAL
ELEMENTS

• **Essential** – These are center-of-the-bullseye elements of our faith. These are 1) truths we must believe in order to be saved, and 2) realities that must be true of us to be saved. For example, we must believe that Jesus is Lord and that he is risen from the dead. It must also be true of us that we have the Holy Spirit and have a faith in Jesus that lasts. Because these are essential to our salvation, they are considered *essentials*.

• **Important** – These are elements of our faith which do not save us, but they are important because they are part of what it means to follow Jesus faithfully. Although the apostle Paul wrote 1 Corinthians to people who were saved (they were clear on the essentials), there were a number of important issues which the Corinthian Christians were needing help with in order to follow Jesus faithfully: church unity, church discipline, and gender confusion, to name a few.

• **Personal** – These are elements of our faith 1) for which we are given freedom to decide based on our own convictions, or 2) for which there is not sufficient direction given in Scripture. For example, the Corinthian Christians were divided as to whether it was okay to eat meat that had originally been part of idolatrous sacrifices. Paul explained in 1 Corinthians 8 that this came down to what an individual's conscience allowed. Act on your conscience in personal matters, but don't let your choices become a stumbling block in another person's relationship with God.

When it comes to matters of church and state, what is essential, important, and personal? We want to suggest the following:

• *Who we are is essential.* Our identity as disciples of King Jesus is nonnegotiable. We are members of Jesus' "body," his church. We are citizens of heaven living as ambassadors of Jesus in whatever corner he places us.

• *What we value is important.* As disciples of Jesus, what we believe and care about need to be formed ever more deeply by the values of Jesus' kingdom. Although we naturally tend to value what helps us get ahead, our values need to be shaped by ongoing discipleship to Jesus.

• *How we vote is personal.*
As we encourage each other

HOW WE VOTE IS PERSONAL.

as fellow disciples of Jesus, we need to give each other space and grace to discern how Jesus' values should inform how we vote. Remember, though: just because how we vote is a "personal element" does not mean that it's inconsequential. These are matters of personal *conviction,* and as such, they need to be the product of prayerful intentionality.

A WARNING

What all this means is that not every battle—political, cultural, or even theological—is a hill worth dying on. That sounds all well and good until you realize that you may have to say no to battles into which other people deeply desire to conscript you.

It might be helpful to note here that, by being strategic about which battles you say *yes* and *no* to, you will likely frustrate three people:

• **Yourself** – It can be personally frustrating knowing that you could be disappointing people by saying no to a fight they find *critical.* Yet it's crucial as followers of Jesus for us to choose our battles wisely and let others fight the rest. We would advocate that it's better to frustrate yourself than to kill yourself trying to fight every cultural battle that presents itself and that others would have you join.

• **Would-be allies** – A lot of people think that "evangelical" is synonymous with a particular way of voting. So, it can be frustrating for the people who thought they could "count you in" or "count on your vote" to realize that they are not your boss. The only one who should be able to lead you like you're a sheep is the Good Shepherd.

• **Would-be enemies** – It can be frustrating for the people who want to hate you to have a more nuanced opponent to reckon with. When dealing with a disciple of Jesus, they may be surprised to find someone who is not reliably an outrage machine and who breaks the narrative with genuine love and intelligent discourse.

In fact, while we're at it, let's add one more person you're going to frustrate by being strategic about which battles you say *yes* and *no* to. You'll frustrate the enemy of our souls. Imagine if you are Holy Spirit-led into crucial spiritual battles—armed with truth, righteousness, the gospel, faith, salvation, the Word of God, and prayer (you can read the whole list of the "armor of God" in Ephesians 6:10–18). Instead of our enemy dealing with a predictable calculator of outrage and anxiety—depending on which buttons he pushes in us—our enemy will realize he's dealing with a warrior.

A disciple of Jesus chooses battles wisely.

ACTION STEPS

1. Reflect on Ephesians 4:1–6. Be sure to take note of what elements are listed as the basis of Christian unity (e.g., one body, one Spirit, one hope, etc.) and think about some things

Christians have fought or attacked each other over that are not included in the list (e.g., masks, immigration reform, etc.)

2. Describe what humility, gentleness, patience, and bearing with each other in love might look like when it comes to political issues and conversations.

8
HOW DO YOU PRAY FOR YOUR NATION?

What part does prayer play in how we interact with politics as a disciple of Jesus? For example, should our prayers go beyond asking God to steer elections in positive directions?

Yes, they should go beyond that. In 1 Timothy 2:1–4, the apostle Paul urged public prayers in church for public leaders. He described these as a practice that "is good and pleases God." He encouraged that we pray "for kings and all those in authority" as a way of seeking peace for everybody and walking in holiness before God. Moreover, Paul reminds us in verse 6 that Jesus "gave himself as a ransom for *all* people," so that even though we should pray for our nation, it is far from the only nation that we should care about or pray for.

Here's 1 Timothy 2:1–4:

"I urge, then, first of all, that petitions, prayers, intercession and thanksgiving be made for all people—for kings and all those in authority, that we may live peaceful and quiet lives in all godliness and holiness. This is good, and pleases God our Savior, who wants all people to be saved and to come to a knowledge of the truth."

Here's what, how, and why we can pray for our nation from 1 Timothy 2:1–4.

WHAT TO PRAY FOR OUR NATION

"All people." Before asking what, from this passage, we can learn about praying for whatever nation we happen to live in, let's pause. This passage zooms out pretty far, far past the boundaries of one nation. From verses 1–6, Paul uses the phrase "all people" three times:

> **PAUL USES THE PHRASE "ALL PEOPLE" THREE TIMES.**

- "I urge, then, first of all, that petitions, prayers, intercession and thanksgiving be made for *all people*." (2:1)
- "God our Savior…wants *all people* to be saved." (2:3b–4a)
- "Christ Jesus…gave himself as a ransom for *all people*." (2:5b–6a)

That said, Paul also encourages us in this passage to pray specifically "for kings and all those in authority, that we may live peaceful and quiet lives." The implication from words like "kings" and "we" is that we're praying for the political leaders in our context.

This would include public officials even up to the highest-tier leaders in our nation ("kings").

And Paul also seems to be encouraging church-wide prayers. Paul's writing this letter to Timothy, the evangelist of the church in Ephesus, and he's writing it to give him instructions on "how people ought to conduct themselves in God's household, which is the church of the living God" (3:15). In 1 Timothy 2, Paul keeps the theme of prayer going, giving further details on how prayer in the public gathering ought to be conducted ("lifting up holy hands without anger or disputing," 2:8).

So, when it comes to these church-wide prayers for national leaders, *what* should we pray? Paul uses four words to describe the types of prayers we ought to pray. Although the first three can function synonymously, there seem to be some shades of nuance in all four words:

- Petitions (Gk. *deesis*) – requesting something in particular
- Prayers (Gk. *proseuche*) – general word for praying
- Intercession (Gk. *enteuxis*) – bringing an appeal on somebody's behalf
- Thanksgiving (Gk. *eucharistia*) – expressing gratitude

That's a pretty vibrant description for the kinds of prayers which, if we do them, can sometimes feel stale and obligatory. "We pray for our leaders, that you would give them wisdom" isn't a bad prayer in itself. But such nuanced words as Paul uses should encourage us to pray with some creativity. Specific requests. Particular names. And let's not miss the very distinctive attitude with which we make these requests: we pray with *thanksgiving* (more on that below). Paul's drawing of our prayers for our leaders is drawn in full color with rich detail.

What do we pray for our nation? We bring God specific requests on behalf of particular people.

HOW TO PRAY FOR OUR NATION

So, *how* do we pray for our nation? Here are some takeaways from 1 Timothy 2:1–4 on how we can pray for the leaders of our nation:

We pray widely. Here's another "all" phrase it can be easy to forget: we are to pray for "all those in authority" (2:2). There are always going to be public officials we have trouble liking. Maybe we feel they're mismanaging their job. Maybe we sense that they oppose our faith. Are we really supposed to pray for *them*? Pray for them to get ousted, sure. But actually pray for *them*?

Really, it's no different from what the New Testament teaches us over and over: It's not our job to select which people are worthy of our love. We are to be like our Father in heaven, "who causes his sun to rise on the evil and the good, and sends rain on the righteous and the unrighteous" (Matthew 5:45b), and that goes for our prayers, as well. To our tendency to get partisan in our prayers, Paul gets persistent with "all…all…all."

We pray gratefully. This one is fascinating. Telling us to pray prayers of "thanksgiving…for kings and all those in authority" can feel strange considering that Paul himself was being constantly *mistreated* by "kings and all those in authority." Here are a few of the things that went terribly wrong for Paul himself because of people in authority (see 2 Corinthians 11:23–29 for the full list):

- Imprisoned multiple times
- 39 lashes (5x)
- Beaten with rods (3x)
- Shipwrecked (3x)
- Pelted with stones

At the time that Paul was writing this list, the first conversion of a Roman emperor to Christianity was still hundreds of years in the future. Paul was telling a persecuted minority to pray prayers of thanksgiving in the context of living under hostile leaders. What an amazing perspective.

We pray peacefully. The church in Ephesus Paul was writing

WE PRAY PEACEFULLY.

to in this letter knew what it was like to be targeted by intolerance and belligerence. When the impact of the gospel began to affect the revenue of idol makers, they retaliated. An influential silversmith lathered a crowd into a riotous mob which became so intense that Paul had to leave the city (Acts 19:23–20:1).

Against this backdrop, it's notable that the prayers Paul urged the Ephesian Christians to pray carried no hint of hitting back. They're peaceful, not pugnacious. We pray "that we may live peaceful and quiet lives." There's evangelism all over this passage (see the next section), but there's no militancy here.

How do we pray for our nation? We pray for our leaders, whether we like them or not, with grateful hearts which desire peace.

WHY WE PRAY FOR OUR NATION

In looking for why we ought to pray for our national leaders, we find a Greek preposition (*ina*) which means "in order that." We offer petitions, prayers, intercession, and thanksgiving for kings and all those in authority in order that (*ina*) "we may live peaceful and quiet lives in all godliness and holiness" (2:2b).

The idea is that, when we're given the freedom to simply be Christians, this peaceful and quiet existence is conducive to our growing in godliness and holiness. Now, it's true that the extreme opposite of persecution—making the church a favored wing of the government—likely results in a compromised, cartoonish church. Somewhere in the middle, there seems to be a sweet spot that Paul is referring to here, where the church can go about its business in quiet and peace. Although the church can grow in astounding ways while persecuted, it would be unwise for us to romanticize the Nero years any more than we should romanticize the Constantine years. As the book of Revelation describes, Satan wields both persecution *and* seduction to try to defeat the church.

Consequently, we are to pray for our nation so that we might live peaceful and quiet lives. But we shouldn't assume that *peaceful* and *quiet* translate to *domesticated* and *privatized*. The ultimate goal—which we see in both this passage and Paul's life mission—is that more and more people will come to faith in Jesus. Paul continues explaining *why* we pray for our nation's leaders:

"…that we may live peaceful and quiet lives in all godliness and holiness. This is good, and pleases God our Savior, who wants all people to be saved and to come to a knowledge of the truth." (1 Timothy 2:2b–4)

Sometimes we're tempted to make *our* nation the one main thing on our minds. As in, if we can just get our political party's platform enacted for a few years, then our nation will be healthy, and we can live satisfied lives. And it's true that seeking the good of our nation *is* in view in this passage; it's reminiscent of Jeremiah 29:7's "Seek the peace and prosperity of the city to which I have carried you." Yet our intent in these prayers is so much bigger and richer than that! Our nation is *far* from the one thing that should be on our minds. In fact, there are *two* "number one's" in 1 Timothy 2:1–4, and neither of them is anything close to a person's nation:

"For there is *one* God and *one* mediator between God and mankind, the man Christ Jesus, who gave himself as a ransom for all people." (2:5–6a)

What ought most to be on our hearts and minds as we pray, hope, strategize, and dream? That God might use us to increase the population of our truest home: heaven.

Why do we pray for our nation? We pray for our nation so that we can live peaceful lives as we carry out our mission of making disciples of all nations.

A disciple of Jesus brings specific requests on behalf of particular people, with grateful hearts which desire peace, with the goal of living peaceful lives and making disciples.

ACTION STEPS

1. Read 1 Timothy 2:1–6a and pray for the governing authorities in your community and of the nation.

2. Create a plan (day of the week, leaders to pray for, etc.) for when and how you will pray for your nation consistently.

9
WHAT'S THE EASIEST SIN IN AN ELECTION YEAR?

When you find yourself in an election year, carve out some time to pause and ask God to take you on a guided tour of your heart. The heart is the source of a lot of evil, often subtle, and politics can make some vices feel necessary, perhaps even virtuous.

Consider the kinds of vices that Jesus said originate in the heart: "For out of the heart come evil thoughts—murder, adultery, sexual immorality, theft, false testimony, slander" (Matthew 15:19). Did you notice slander on the same list as murder, adultery, sexual immorality, and theft? Take note of that. Murder is taking someone's life. Adultery is taking someone's spouse. Sexual immorality is taking someone's purity. Theft is taking someone's possessions. What does slander take? It is taking someone's name and stomping it into the dirt.

Slander is the easiest sin for people to commit in an election year. Slander is telling lies about others meant to hurt them. Careless overstatement—whether glossing over history, flattering allies, or slandering opponents—becomes as easy in an election year as gluttony at an all-you-can-eat buffet. This overstatement includes slander toward politicians you don't agree with, toward anyone who supports those politicians, and toward fellow Christians who don't denounce those politicians strongly enough. Attack ads and debate zingers, amplified by social media algorithms, attempt to fling enough mud to brand the opponent as grotesque and villainous.

Slander is a coward twice over. It's usually done behind the back *and* with other people, so that

SLANDER IS A COWARD TWICE OVER.

it's at least two people ganging up on another person behind his or her back. Yet, being cowardly doesn't make slander any less dangerous. Cruel words may be small, but as James tells us, they are the same kind of small as a lit match in a forest, a bit in a horse's mouth, a rudder on a ship, and a dose of poison (see James 3). As David Livingstone Smith describes in his book *Less Than Human: Why We Demean, Enslave, and Exterminate Others*, using the word "rat" in reference to Jews fueled the Holocaust, using "savage beast" in reference to Native Americans justified their exploitation by Europeans, and using "cockroach" by one African tribe in reference to another made the Rwandan genocide of 1994 conscionable.[17]

SLANDER BY CHRISTIANS

Sadly, Christians have not been immune to slandering their ideological opponents. Sometimes, the slander is a matter of misrepresenting other religions in unflattering ways (e.g., misrepresenting Buddhism as a violent religion or Muslims as moon worshipers or Jews as blood-drinking child killers).

[17] David Livingstone Smith, *Less Than Human: Why We Demean, Enslave, and Exterminate Others* (New York: St. Martin's Press, 2011).

Perhaps just as often, Christians slander each other, whether it's the Roman Catholics calling the Lollards "false and perverse people . . . [who ought to be] utterly destroyed"[18] or mainstream Protestants feeling justified in despising, persecuting, and even killing Anabaptists in the decades following the Reformation. There was truth in the pagan Roman Emperor Julian's exaggerated observation that "No wild beasts are as dangerous to men as Christians are to each other."[19] There was also some truth in in Jewish philosopher Benedict Spinoza's claim that Christians "quarrel with such rancorous animosity and display daily towards one another such bitter hatred, that this, rather than the virtues which they profess, is the readiest criteria of their faith."[20]

Scripture does not vacillate on whether slander is okay for the people of God. Scripture is unanimous and insistent: "Whoever conceals hatred with lying lips and spreads slander is a fool" (Proverbs 10:18). Do you want to dwell with God? You will need to be counted among those "whose tongue utters no slander, who does no wrong to a neighbor, and casts no slur on others" (Psalm 15:3). The celebrated "love your neighbor" passage in Leviticus is set in the context of never endangering your neighbor's life as well as never going about "spreading slander among your people" (Leviticus 19:16).

Disciples of Jesus must "get rid of all bitterness, rage and anger, brawling and slander, along with every form of malice" (Ephesians 4:31). If we could somehow switch out the first letter of each word in "all bitterness, rage, anger, brawling, slander, and malice" to spell

---

[18] "De Haeretico Comburendo, 1401," in *Documents of the Christian Church*, 4th edition, edited by Henry Bettenson and Chris Maunder (Oxford: Oxford University Press, 2011), 191–192.

[19] Julianus Augustus, quoted in Ammianus Marcellinus, *Roman Antiquities*, Book XXII, chapter 5, https://penelope.uchicago.edu/Thayer/E/Roman/Texts/Ammian/22*.html.

[20] Benedict Spinoza, quoted in Douglas J. Moo, *The Letter of James* (Grand Rapids: Wm. B. Eerdmans Publishing Co., 2000), 181.

POLITICS, we would have the perfect acronym. Yet for the Christian, these aren't options even in an election year. Somehow, in an election year we must seek truth, pursue justice, and walk in conviction—even while flinging away bitterness, rage, anger, brawling, slander, and malice as soon as they creep into our consciousness. Christians don't fling mud onto people. Even when it's thrown at us, we can fling it onto the floor. Jesus' "turn the other cheek" was another way of telling us never to respond to insult with insult.

SLANDER TOWARD CHRISTIANS

If slander is lies meant to hurt, we Christians get slandered regularly. And so did the early

CHRISTIANS GET SLANDERED REGULARLY.

church. They were falsely accused of blasphemy (Acts 6:11), lawlessness (Acts 6:13; 18:13), sedition (Acts 17:6–7), temple defilement (Acts 21:28), and rioting (Acts. 24:5–6). Christians have known slander from the beginning, and it didn't stop in the book of Acts. We read in other books of the next centuries of how Christians were called atheistic (not believing in the numerous Roman gods), incestuous (loving each other as "brother" and "sister"), and even cannibalistic (celebrating a feast involving the body and blood of their leader).

In such manner, people slandered Jesus, his apostles, and the early church. And increasingly our culture is slandering us—recording and publishing statements about us that are not true and are hurtful. They can give us labels that don't fit, but yet still stick and still sting—labels meant to make us look like idiots and feel like bigots. And it usually gets worse in an election year.

FIVE CHRISTIAN RESPONSES TO SLANDER

It doesn't look like slander against Christians will be stopping anytime soon. It's been a thing for a couple thousand years, and it seems to be rising in the increasingly post-Christian Western world. Especially when it comes to Christian ethical stances which interface with politics, we can be called bigoted and hateful when we try to ground our beliefs about sexuality, marriage, gender, and human life in what God teaches us in the Bible. The New Testament shows us five responses that Christians ought to have when slandered. Since misrepresentation is not going away anytime soon, let's learn these responses and practice them:

1. Look back and remember our spiritual ancestors.

As we look back over biblical history, we see many of our spiritual ancestors slandered for their faith. Far from being something strange, being slandered can be an indicator that we're on the right track. Here's how Jesus put it:

> "Blessed are you when people insult you, persecute you and falsely say all kinds of evil against you because of me. Rejoice and be glad, because great is your reward in heaven, for in the same way they persecuted the prophets who were before you." (Matthew 5:11–12)

"Falsely say all kinds of evil against you because of me" is the best definition of anti-Christian slander a person could find. Isaiah, Jeremiah, Ezekiel, Daniel—these prophets all got slandered and mistreated because of their faith. People didn't want to hear the truth back then. A lot of people don't want to hear the truth now. Getting slandered is no walk in the park, but it should not come as a surprise. Accordingly, we encourage you as believers to look back and remember with gratitude those who kept following God because they focused on his voice calling them forward, instead of on the voices calling them to drop out.

2. Look ahead and live honorably.

Since we know that slander is going to try and attach to us, we can look ahead and try to prevent the slander from sticking. How do we do this? By living honorably. By doing what is good and right. The apostle Peter gave this encouragement:

> "Live such good lives among the pagans that, though they accuse you of doing wrong, they may see your good deeds and glorify God on the day he visits us." (1 Peter 2:12)

By your words or your actions, you can make hurtful lies about Christians implausible. This is because people who have come to know you know from experience that you're not a bigot or an idiot. Look ahead, know that slander may come, and live in such an honest and honorable way that the slander will not stick.

3. Look within and remind ourselves that Jesus is Lord.

When you are slandered for your faith in Jesus, it's an opportunity to pause, look into your heart, and remind yourself why you're following Jesus in the first place. It's a critical time to remind yourself that *Jesus is Lord.* Peter explained it this way:

> "But even if you should suffer for what is right, you are blessed. 'Do not fear their threats; do not be frightened.' But in your hearts revere Christ as Lord. Always be prepared to give an answer to everyone who asks you to give the reason for the hope that you have. But do this with gentleness and respect, keeping a clear conscience, so that those who speak maliciously against your good behavior in Christ may be ashamed of their slander." (1 Peter 3:14–16)

4. Look out there and show kindness.

How should we feel about the people who slander us? When we look out there at our slanderers, what should be our response? According to Paul,

> "To this very hour we go hungry and thirsty, we are in rags, we are brutally treated, we are homeless. We work hard with our own hands. When we are cursed, we bless; when we are persecuted, we endure it; when we are slandered, we answer kindly." (1 Corinthians 4:11–13a)

WHEN WE ARE CURSED, WE BLESS.

Why respond to our slanderers with kindness? It's because, when we were God's enemies, he showed kindness to us. We're passing along what we've received.

5. Look up and trust God.

When we find ourselves lied about, labeled unfairly, or treated unkindly, it's time to look up and pray. After Peter and John were jailed overnight for healing a person and preaching about Jesus, they were let out with a warning not to preach any longer in Jesus' name. When Peter and John returned to their fellow Christians, they prayed this prayer:

> "Sovereign Lord, you made the heavens and the earth and the sea, and everything in them. You spoke by the Holy Spirit through the mouth of your servant, our father David: 'Why do the nations rage and the peoples plot in vain?' . . . Now, Lord, consider their threats and enable your servants to speak your word with great boldness." (Acts 4:24b–25, 29)

Facing slander and threats, they asked God for confidence and kept trusting him. The result of their prayer: "After they prayed, the place where they were meeting was shaken. And they were all filled with the Holy Spirit and spoke the word of God boldly" (Acts 4:31).

A disciple of Jesus responds to slander with trust in God and kindness toward others.

ACTION STEPS

1. Reflect on Luke 6:27–30 and 1 Peter 3:8–9. What do these passages teach you about responding to slander?

2. Think through a straightforward plan for becoming the kind of person who can "bless and curse not." What are 2–3 habits or disciplines you can do in partnership with the Spirit to become this kind of person?

PART 2 – QUESTIONS ABOUT DILEMMAS & DECISIONS

10
HOW DO YOU FIGURE OUT WHAT'S RIGHT AND WRONG AS A CHRISTIAN?

The final book in C. S. Lewis's children's fantasy series The Chronicles of Narnia is *The Last Battle*. In it, a donkey named Puzzle is tricked by an ape named Shift into wearing a lionskin they found and pretending to be the great lion Aslan. By bringing "Aslan" out to make appearances, Shift feeds the simpleminded donkey lines to say, so that the inhabitants of Narnia do Shift's bidding while thinking they are obeying commands from Aslan. As Narnia descends into chaos, Puzzle the donkey knows something is wrong. Yet he continues to tell himself what an unintelligent donkey he is, so there isn't anything he can do about it. Later in the story, one main character wishes aloud to Puzzle, "If you'd spent less time saying you weren't clever and more time trying to be as clever as you could . . ."[21]

Society's descent into chaos can cue Christians to brood and say, "Well, I'm not clever enough to do anything about it." Intellectual apathy can lead us to bury our intellect in the sand and hop on the

---

[21] C. S. Lewis, *The Last Battle* (New York: Scholastic, Inc., 1995), 95.

next colorful bandwagon that happens by. What's needed from all of us is praying hard, thinking well, and doing what we can to be an outpost of heaven in our corner of the world. There are plenty of Shifts eager to coopt our voices. If we want our voices to speak truth and not propaganda, we need to step up and be the best thinkers we can be.

So, how do you figure out what's right and wrong as a disciple of Jesus?

WHY THIS IS IMPORTANT

Before getting to the how, let's pause and ask why. Why is it important for Christians to pause and think deeply about what's right and wrong? First, because God warns us against mistaking good for evil: "Woe to those who call evil good and good evil , who put darkness for light and light for

> **WOE TO THOSE WHO CALL EVIL GOOD AND GOOD EVIL.**

darkness, who put bitter for sweet and sweet for bitter" (Isaiah 5:20). God cares that we don't do wrong *and* that we don't approve of what's wrong. After listing numerous vices, such as sexual sin, greed, envy, and slander, Paul laments about those who "not only continue to do these very things but also approve of those who practice them" (Romans 1:32b).

There's another reason we need to be diligent in discerning what's right and wrong. The atheist existentialist Friedrich Nietzsche was correct when he described a "transvaluation of all values" that would happen when Western culture no longer took God seriously. When we no longer care about what God thinks, our values shift.

Vices will become virtues and virtues vices. Here are some examples of this trickle-down transvaluation in contemporary Western culture, according to which objective goods are transformed into evils:

- Objective truth – a fantasy created by powerful people to maintain power
- Biblical morality – a set of outdated, repressive, and destructive instructions
- Monogamous marriage – an institution which domesticates women as property
- Chastity – an unrealistic, harmful, and bland restriction of sexuality which benefits domineering, heterosexual men
- Christian evangelism/missions – a form of spiritual imperialism
- Sanctity of human life – a way for religious people to control women's bodies

Objective truth, biblical morality, monogamous marriage—each one of these help people flourish in countless ways. Yet each one of them, in modern Western culture, are being labeled as poison. This is because the Devil is a taker, not a maker. He takes what is good and mislabels it. He makes us cynical toward the things which help us and save us.

In this climate of transvaluation, Christians must pray hard and think well about what's right and wrong.

WHAT MAKES IT COMPLICATED

Let's start with a very simple truth. When it comes to the basics, you and I know what's right and wrong. If you've got a Bible, you know God's moral laws. If you *don't* have a Bible, you know God's moral laws. This is because, for everyone, "the requirements of the law are written on their hearts, their consciences also bearing witness, and their thoughts sometimes accusing them and at other times even defending them" (Romans 2:15). We all have a sense that murder, theft, adultery, and dishonesty are morally wrong, even if we might argue that they are justified from time to time in our special circumstances.

Yet, beyond the basics, it can get hard to discern what is right and wrong.

Sometimes two objectively good things conflict with each other, and we have to figure out which is more important than the other. For example, human life *and* bodily autonomy are both objectively important, but you must prioritize one over the other when it comes to whether it's ethical to have an abortion. Should we recognize more value in the life of the preborn baby or in the autonomy of the woman over what's inside her body?

> SOMETIMES TWO OBJECTIVELY GOOD THINGS CONFLICT.

Other times, we can agree on an objectively good goal, but we can't agree on the best way to get there. Let's say we both agree that human life is sacred and thus can't be taken. Ironically, that might be the reason one of us favors capital punishment for murder *and* the reason the other says capital punishment is not ethical—

because it takes human life. Or we can both agree that people in poverty ought not to remain in poverty, while one of us believes free market capitalism is the way to alleviate poverty, while the other of us prescribes governmental interventions as the way to help the poor.

And, as already, mentioned, another major complication in knowing right from wrong is that the Devil is actively (and successfully) trying to brand virtues as vices and vices as virtues.

WAYS PEOPLE DETERMINE WHAT'S RIGHT AND WRONG

If you've taken an ethics class or had an ethics section in a philosophy class, you've probably learned terms such as virtue ethics, deontological ethics, utilitarianism, and ethical egoism. These theories disagree with each other, but taken together, they helpfully point us to three major ways of figuring out what is right and wrong. They all start with the letter C:

- **Character** – We make our best ethical decisions when we are people of virtue who value the right things.
- **Commands** – There are ethical rules (e.g., God's commands) which give us direction in what decisions to make.
- **Consequences** – When making ethical decisions, it is helpful to think through what good and bad consequences will follow the decision.

Although these C words could be turned against each other, as Christians, it is best to discern how they can fit together to help us make ethical decisions. Our best decisions arise from God's *character*

("You are a people holy to the Lord" [Deuteronomy 7:6a]), follow God's *commands* ("Take care to follow the commands" [Deuteronomy 7:11a]), and result in good *consequences* for ourselves and others ("If you pay attention to these laws and are careful to follow them. . . you will be blessed more than any other people" [Deuteronomy 7:14a]). Consider the following passage, and ask yourself which C is represented by the bold, which C is represented by the italics, and which C is represented by the underline:

> "Finally, all of you, **be** like-minded, **be** sympathetic, *love* one another, **be** compassionate and humble. *Do not repay* evil with evil or insult with insult. On the contrary, *repay* evil with blessing, because to this you were called <u>so that</u> you may inherit a blessing." (1 Peter 3:8–9)

We see character in the bolded words, commands in the italicized words, and consequences in the underlined words. All three have their place for the disciple of Jesus in discovering what's right and wrong.

A FRAMEWORK FOR DISCOVERING YOUR POSITION ON ___

Now, hang on. This all sounds like work. Wouldn't it be better to simply have a list which gives the biblical stamp of approval or disapproval on each of the major ethical questions? *Right. Wrong. Right. Wrong. Wrong.* Wouldn't a list of right and wrong actions be better—and more biblical—than learning a framework for discovering your own position on issues?

Actually, the Bible does give us this kind of clear-cut direction on many issues. As one example, Paul in 1 Corinthians 6:9–10 gives us a list of sins which, if regularly practiced without repentance, will keep someone from inheriting God's kingdom: sexual immorality, idolatry, adultery, homosexuality, theft, greed, drunkenness, slander, and fraud. It's not at all an oversimplification for Christians to look at such a list and label each as a sin.

However, many contemporary questions are not directly dealt with in Scripture. Is it right or wrong for a Christian to attend a friend's gay wedding? Can a disciple of Jesus smoke weed? What about abortifacient methods of birth control? Non-abortifacient methods? Should Christians give to panhandlers? Is gambling a sin? Is cremation a valid option for Christian burial? Is it right or wrong to use a transgender person's preferred pronouns? Is it okay for a Christian to serve in active duty if that might mean taking a life? When something is a sin according to Scripture, that doesn't automatically mean that we should want it to be criminalized, but is there a level of destructiveness at which a sin should be made illegal by the government?

You might assume that some or all of these questions have quick, easy answers straight out of the Bible. But they don't. Finding our guidance from Scripture, however, we *can* come to biblical, thoughtful, God-honoring positions on these questions. We

WE CAN COME TO BIBLICAL, THOUGHTFUL, GOD-HONORING POSITIONS.

want to propose a framework for how you can do this. They involve the three Cs mentioned above.

• **Character** – What virtues and values should guide your view on this ethical issue?

• **Commands** – What dos and do nots should guide your view on this ethical issue?

• **Consequences** – What consequences do you intend to happen (and not happen) by how you hold your view on this ethical issue?

When it comes to a certain ethical issue, it will be fruitful to walk through the three Cs. After doing so, we encourage you to articulate your view by filling in the following blanks:

"As a person who ___ (fill in with character), I will obey ___ (fill in with commands) by ___ (fill in with your decision/ view) in such a way that ___ (fill in with the consequences you intend to happen)."

Although we will flesh this framework out in greater detail in future chapters, here is one example of how it might look applied to pornography:

"As a person of faithfulness and self-control (Galatians 5:22– 23) who values all people as God's image bearers (Genesis 1:27) [*character*], I will obey Scripture's commands to love my wife (Ephesians 5:25), to honor my marriage (Hebrews 13:4), to treat young women as sisters with absolute purity (1 Timothy 5:2), and not to look at a person with lust (Matthew 5:27–30) [*commands*], by making it a personal rule to fully abstain from porn (on websites, magazines, etc.) and from watching nude scenes in movies [*decision*], in such a way that my devotion to my wife isn't compromised and my thoughts are better able to focus on what is noble and pure (Philippians 4:8) [*consequences*]."

In future chapters, we will guide you in applying this framework to multiple ethical questions in order to discover thoughtful, biblical positions. We believe you will find this thought exercise worthwhile as you pray hard and think well about tough ethical questions in our contemporary world.

A disciple of Jesus imitates Christ's character by obeying his commands, and the results are good consequences, whether in this life or the next.

ACTION STEPS

1. Read Romans 12:1–2. What is the difference between being conformed and being transformed? According to this passage, how are we transformed?

2. The religious leaders of Jesus' day frequently asked Jesus to weigh in on the hot button debates of the day, and a lot of times Jesus responded by saying something like, "Have you

not read . . . ." And then he'd quote a passage of Scripture. This reminds us how important it is to continually read and reflect on the Bible so that we can see things more the way God wants us to. In fact, sociological studies have shown that nominal Christians are actually worse for society than secular people. So, what is your plan to read and reflect on the Bible so you can grow in thinking like Jesus?

11
WHAT VIRTUES AND VALUES SHOULD FORM YOU AS YOU VOTE?

The novel *1984*, written in 1949 by George Orwell, is about a "Big Brother" government. In this book, the government controls everything about everyone's life, even down to the last detail of controlling what people think and believe. No freedom whatsoever. The novel centers on two characters named *Winston* and *Julia*, who are citizens of this totalitarian regime and who have had enough of Big Brother. They're ready for freedom, they talk and dream of freedom, but they're not sure how they can attain it.

Winston and Julia are not sure whom they can trust, but they think they can trust an official named O'Brien. They secretly approach *O'Brien*, and sure enough O'Brien reveals to them that he is part of the "resistance," the secret group who will try to overthrow Big Brother. He asks them a series of questions to test their loyalty to the resistance. O'Brien asks Winston and Julia, "You are prepared to give your lives?" Yes.

"You are prepared to commit murder?" Yes. "To commit acts of sabotage which may cause the death of hundreds of innocent people?" Yes. "You are prepared to cheat, to forge, to blackmail, to corrupt the minds of children, to distribute habit-forming drugs . . . to do anything which is likely to cause demoralization and weaken the power of the Party?" Yes. "If, for example, it would somehow serve our interests to throw sulphuric acid in a child's face—are you prepared to do that?" Yes.

By the end of the questions, Winston and Julia are officially a part of the resistance. O'Brien then dismisses them and lets them know they will hear from him soon. And they do. Shortly after their conversation with O'Brien, Winston and Julia are arrested. They have been discovered. It got found out that they were trying to overthrow Big Brother. How did the authorities find out? The answer is, O'Brien. He was never part of the resistance. O'Brien was always just a clever official for Big Brother.

After Winston is arrested, it is O'Brien who is put in charge of his torture and reeducation. During one conversation, Winston is weakening, but he's still trying to convince O'Brien that Winston is right in his convictions, and that the Big Brother machine is wrong and evil. O'Brien asks, "And you consider yourself morally superior to us, with our lies and our cruelty?"

"Yes, I consider myself superior," answers Winston.

Without saying a word, O'Brien starts playing a recording, a recording that Winston instantly remembers: "You are prepared to commit murder?" Yes. "To commit acts of sabotage which may cause the death of hundreds of innocent people?" Yes. Cheat, forge, blackmail, corrupt, acid. Yes, yes, yes. And Winston realizes that with all those yeses, he has lost all his credibility.

Christians, too, lose credibility with a series of yeses. Yes to shrinking Christ's church into the religious arm of a political party. Yes

> **CHRISTIANS, TOO, LOSE CREDIBILITY WITH A SERIES OF YESES.**

to misplaced trust in political saviors. Yes to gaining electoral victories in exchange for losing souls. Yes to nothing but hatred for political enemies and nothing but praise for political allies. Yes to useful idiocy instead of prophetic critique.

This sort of drunken stagger toward incredibility starts with *forgetfulness*. We forget the virtues and values that form us as disciples of Jesus.

SHOULD WE START WITH CONSEQUENCES, COMMANDS, OR CHARACTER?

Remember the three Cs from the last chapter? When it comes to how people decide right from wrong, there are three ways they typically do it:

Character

Commands

Consequences

Consider the stair-like appearance of our consequences-commands-character framework. If these were literal steps made of concrete, which step would contain the most concrete? As the longest step, consequences would. This is helpful to remember, since consequences are a very "concrete" way of reasoning. You can visualize specific consequences based on this or that political position. If your nation is on the brink of war, you can envision the casualties and develop your stance based on those consequences.

Up from there, commands/rules are less "concrete." It's easy to see a command—take for example the biblical command, "Do not let the sun go down while you are still angry" (Ephesians 4:26b)—and say, "Well, sure, in a general sense, I should do that, but it just wouldn't work out in my specific situation."

Finally, let's look at character. Making decisions based on character is the least "concrete" of all. When it comes to decisions involving politics, it's true, but fairly vague, to say, "Well, you need to think through what it means to be kind, compassionate, and fair, and then vote that way."

When it comes to ethical issues that interface with politics, the most natural place to start is with *consequences*. Because consequences are so "concrete," they can be easier to argue from. Here are some examples of consequential reasoning: "Open borders are immoral because migrant influx overwhelms our infrastructure." "Fossil fuels need to be phased out to stabilize the climate." "We shouldn't legalize physician-assisted suicide because it will lead to active euthanasia." "Marijuana legalization will not affect you." Do you notice the common thread through all these statements? The argument is that a given issue is okay or not okay based on the good or bad consequences that follow.

Although consequence arguments are more concrete, they also easily lead to impasse. This is because the consequences one person fears might be different from the consequences another person fears.

Perhaps one of us fears how marijuana legalization might further impair our youth, while the other fears how its criminalization fills prisons with nonviolent offenders. It's often when our consequentialist arguments come to an impasse that one of us goes up a step in ethical argumentation—by bringing in a command/rule or two.

As Christians, perhaps we bring in a command from Scripture. For example, if we're disagreeing about whether capital punishment will lead to better or worse consequences, one of us might bring in a command from Scripture—say, Genesis 9:6a: "Whoever sheds human blood, by humans shall their blood be shed." Then the other of us might bring in their own biblical command, for example, showing from Micah 6:8 that God requires us "to act justly *and* to love mercy."

We want to suggest that, for disciples of Jesus, it's not a good idea to start our ethical reasoning with consequences or commands. Yes, both consequences and commands are crucial, and we will get to them. But they're not the best *starting* point. Starting with consequences makes it too easy to forget about God's role in helping us know right from wrong. Even starting with God's commands can make it too easy for us to be selective and find loopholes. In the Sermon on the Mount, Jesus walked through Old Testament commands which people had technically "obeyed" while missing the heart of the commands. For example,

> "You have heard that it was said, 'You shall not commit adultery.' But I tell you that anyone who looks at a woman lustfully has already committed adultery with her in his heart." (Matthew 5:27–28)

Jesus wants us to start with the *heart*. Of first importance is character—that is, our virtues and

> ## JESUS WANTS US TO START WITH THE HEART.

values. When we do not start there, we can get selective and find loopholes. Not starting with character means eventually losing our credibility.

CONTEMPLATING THE VIRTUES AND VALUES OF JESUS

So, what virtues and values should form us as we vote? As for virtues, well, *all* of them. Throughout Scripture, we find there are many virtues which God cultivates in his people. For example, "The fruit of the Spirit is love, joy, peace, forbearance, kindness, goodness, faithfulness, gentleness and self-control" (Galatians 5:22–23a). We find more lists of virtues (what we are to "be") in passages such as Romans 12 and Colossians 3.

As for values, since we're disciples of Jesus, let's narrow it down to *his* values. It's worthwhile to go through a Gospel and ask throughout, "What does Jesus value here?" Learning to value what Jesus values is challenging and transformative.

Again, we don't start with consequences or commands (although we'll get there). We start with cultivating the character of Christ—his virtues and values. And we start cultivating his character by contemplating him: "And we all, who with unveiled faces contemplate the Lord's glory, are being transformed into his image with ever-increasing glory, which comes from the Lord, who is the Spirit" (2 Corinthians 3:18).

Let's contemplate Jesus' glory through this list of value statements we glean from the first few chapters of the Gospel of Matthew (for a fuller list, see appendix A). In each of these passages, Jesus models what should win over what in our value system. Just think of a game of rock, paper, scissors; Jesus is teaching us what's "rock" and what's "scissors."

3:13–15	Doing what is righteous over what makes most sense
4:1	Spirit-led over comfortable
4:3–4	Spiritual needs (e.g., our need for God's words) over physical comfort
4:5–10	Right way over easy way
4:18–19	Eternal needs over physical needs
5:11–12	Reward in heaven over comforts of earth
5:14–16	Being a light over blending in
5:20	Righteousness of the heart over technical obedience
5:23–24	Reconciliation over religious rituals
5:27–30	Heaven over pleasures of sin
5:32	Faithfulness in marriage over the easy way out
5:33–37	Doing what you say you'll do over making elaborate promises
5:38–42	The other person's salvation over your rights
5:43–48	Loving our enemies over just loving friends
6:1	Acts of righteousness for God over getting noticed by people
6:2–4	Reward in heaven over applause on earth
6:5–8	Authenticity in prayer over fancy words
6:16–18	Sincerity over putting on a show

6:19–21   Treasures in heaven over stuff of earth

6:24   Serving God over making money

6:25–34   Trust in God over worrying about stuff

6:26–27   Content in my worth over busying myself with worry

6:33   Seeking God's kingdom over meeting our needs

7:1–2   Showing mercy to others over mainly giving yourself mercy

7:3–5   Self-examination over always needing to fix other people's problems

7:7–8   Trusting in God's providence over keeping distance from God

7:12   Treating others the way you want to be treated over just treating yourself

7:13–14   Traveling the narrow path over settling for the easy path

7:15–20   Watching out for false prophets over complacently assuming the best

7:21–23   Doing our Father's will over doing impressive things for God

7:24–27   Following Jesus' teachings over just hearing Jesus' teachings

8:1–3   Showing mercy in personal ways over just helping from a distance

8:10–12   Having faith in Jesus' abilities over being born in the right group

8:19–22   The urgency of following Jesus over physical and family interests

8:24–26   Faith during a storm over panic during a storm

8:28–34   Helping the hurting over maintaining the peaceful status quo

9:1–8   Having our sins forgiven over being healed (the latter is seen here as confirmation of the former)

9:9–13   Hanging out with sinners over impressing the righteous

9:14–17   Celebrating Jesus' presence over maintaining old religious traditions

9:18–26   Our faith in Jesus' ability over our contentedness to leave Jesus alone

9:35–38   Compassion for the hurting (becoming a harvest worker) over living typical lives

If we really want to learn how to represent Jesus in how we live, engage, and vote, we won't start with consequences or commands (although those will come, too). We will start with contemplating the character of Christ.

WHERE WE'RE GOING

So, here's where we're going next. We'll begin internalizing a framework that we can apply to the ethical issues that shape how we live and vote. Here's the framework, starting with character as we learn it from Jesus:

"As a person who ___ (fill in with character), I will obey ___ (fill in with commands) by ___ (fill in with your view) in such a way that ___ (fill in with consequences)."

In the next chapter, we'll begin applying this framework to the question of how we figure out what's true.

A disciple of Jesus gains and keeps credibility by making decisions rooted in the virtues and values of Jesus.

ACTION STEP

1. Read over the list of Jesus' values again (for a fuller list, see appendix A), and pick 7–10 values that stand out to and challenge you. Read the verses associated with each and reflect on what it would look like for you to embody that value in your context, as Jesus did in his.

12
WHAT DOES CHRISTIANITY TEACH ABOUT THE TRUTH?

Raising toddler boys is a blast—but sometimes it also gives parents a front-row seat to the art of creative misuse. Toddler boys' strong imaginations teach us that anything can be used as anything other than what it's supposed to be used for. A plate might become a frisbee. Permanent markers become crayons—for walls. Indoor plants become buried treasure to uproot and dig up. Anything long and pointy becomes a sword, which can make outdoor hikes last a long time because every stick needs to be picked up and examined for its swordsiness.

Creative misuse is entertaining when coming from toddler boys—not so much when grown-ups try it. When it comes to creative misuse, we can all become like toddler boys with one of God's greatest gifts: *truth.*

You might have met some preacher's kids (PKs) who turned out pretty rough, but you've never met a PK who turned out as unchristian as Friedrich Nietzsche. As the son of a Lutheran minister, he eventually became an atheist who despised Christian morality and eagerly heralded a post-Christian world. Nietzsche had his faults, but *inconsistency* was not one of them. He reasoned very logically that with the "death of God" came the death of absolute morality and truth (the "transvaluation" we described in chapter 10).

Eager to hurry on through God's supposed funeral, Nietzsche excitedly anticipated the newfound ability of dominant humans (Nietzsche's "overman") to recreate reality in their own image. It is a matter of erasing the concept of truth and artistically redrawing reality. It's no wonder that the only line in the New Testament which Nietzsche appreciated was when Pontius Pilate scoffed, "What is truth?"[22]

Although, sadly, he died insane, Nietzsche's predictive powers were remarkably incisive. Modern Western culture has become a playground for powerful people to recreate reality to mirror their desires.

How do we as disciples of Jesus not follow our culture into creative misuse of the truth? The way not to misuse truth is to seek truth in order that we might live in it. The Gospel of John pictures living in truth as bringing our whole selves into the light. Sin thrives in the darkness but withers in the light. Lies mutate and spread in the darkness but evaporate in the light.

Living in the light means more than merely amassing pieces of truth to get smarter or win debates. It's a matter of welcoming the truth—the whole truth—by being disciples of the one who is "the way, the truth, and the life" (John 14:6). Here is your central choice when it comes to what you're going to do with the truth:

---

[22] Friedrich Nietzsche, *The Antichrist*, translated by H. L. Mencken (New York: Alfred. A. Knopf, 1920), 134–135.

"Everyone who does evil hates the light, and will not come into the light for fear that their deeds will be exposed. But whoever lives by the truth comes into the light." (John 3:20–21)

> **WHOEVER LIVES BY THE TRUTH COMES INTO THE LIGHT.**

Let's walk through the following steps in order to respond to real-life dilemmas related to truth.

WHICH OPTION DO YOU TEND TO CHOOSE WHEN IT COMES TO TRUTH?

1. I absorb my beliefs from the people around me or over me, without checking whether they're true or not.
2. I create truth because I am my own highest authority. I have just as much right to create reality as anyone else, including God.
3. I seek truth from God and seek to live by it whether it's convenient or not.

WHAT DO THE FOLLOWING SCRIPTURES TEACH YOU ABOUT TRUTH?

Jeremiah 9:3–9	
John 8:31–32	
Romans 1:18–25	
1 Corinthians 13:6	

PICK A REAL-LIFE DILEMMA WHEN IT COMES TO TRUTH (HERE ARE SOME EXAMPLES):

1. Will I use a person's "preferred pronouns" when they go against the person's biological sex? *Genesis 1:26–27; Ephesians 4:14–15.*

2. Will I continue to regularly tune into news/commentary from a news outlet if I sense that it is deliberately making me angry and fearful (over being clear-headed)? *Colossians 3:8; Philippians 4:4–8.*

3. When I take a stand against a political party because of some vice (e.g., from one of its leaders), will I be consistent in standing against the same vice when it's in my own preferred political party? *Proverbs 26:28; James 2:9.*

WHAT CHRISTLIKE CHARACTER TRAITS (VIRTUES AND VALUES) OUGHT TO INFORM YOUR RESPONSE TO THE DILEMMA? (FEEL FREE TO LOOK BACK AT CHAPTER 11 OR AHEAD AT APPENDIX A FOR A LIST OF JESUS' VALUES FROM THE GOSPEL OF MATTHEW.)

WHAT COMMANDS OF SCRIPTURE (DOS AND DON'TS) OUGHT TO INFORM YOUR RESPONSE TO THE DILEMMA?

WHAT CONSEQUENCES DO YOU INTEND TO HAPPEN (AND NOT HAPPEN) AS A RESULT OF YOUR DECISION/VIEW?

FILL IN THE BLANKS:

As a person of ____ (fill in with virtues) who values ____ (fill in with values),

I will obey ___ (fill in with commands)

by ___ (fill in with your decision/view)

in such a way that ___ (fill in with consequences).

13
WHAT DOES CHRISTIANITY TEACH ABOUT THE BEDROOM?

C. S. Lewis said that when you're the captain of a ship, you've got to keep in mind three things.[23] First, if you're in formation with other ships, make sure you're not ramming them. Play well with others. Second, how's your ship doing? Is it in ship shape? Third, are you going where you're supposed to be going? This is the big-picture question: are you going the right direction to the right destination?

As Lewis explains, that's a good checklist of our ethics, too. Are you getting along with others? Are you healthy yourself? Are you heading to the right destination?

When it comes to sexual ethics, which of those three ethical questions matters most to most people in our contemporary world? It's the first question: how your sexual behavior affects other people. Most people think that whatever two consenting adults do is fine—so long as it does not hurt anyone. "Love is love." Along the way, what are most people forgetting? The second and third questions: "Are you

---

[23] C. S. Lewis, Mere Christianity (New York: HarperCollins, 2001), 71–72.

morally healthy?" and "Is your life going the right direction to the right destination?" What the Bible calls "sexual immorality" is not helping you out, and it's also not helping you go the right direction to the right destination.

Christians have historically believed that, since God invented sexuality, he gets to define what

GOD INVENTED SEXUALITY.

it's for. But what if I really want something that God calls "sexual immorality"? In fact, what if it's almost a compulsion? What if the way I'm wired sets me up to really want what God calls "sexual immorality"?

There was once a college student regularly sleeping around, whose pastor confronted him about his sexual sin. "I can't stop," the student told his pastor.

The pastor painted a hypothetical scenario. "Tell you what. Let's say things are starting to heat up between you and your sexual partner. I come to your door, knock, and you come to the door. I say, 'Listen. If you don't go through with this, I'll give you a hundred bucks.' What would you choose?"

The student says, "I'd take the hundred bucks and stop."

Why?

Even when you really want something sexually, it is possible to have a *higher* desire.

As disciples of Jesus, our overriding desire is to follow Christ, which at times is going to be highly counter-cultural. Just as Christian sexual ethics has been in its wider context, since its birth into the Greco-Roman world.

Let's walk through the following steps in order to respond to real-life dilemmas related to the bedroom.

WHICH OPTION DO YOU TEND TO CHOOSE WHEN IT COMES TO SEXUALITY?

1. "I believe that what people do sexually is fine as long as it doesn't hurt anyone. The Bible's prohibitions regarding premarital sex, homosexual sex, and multiple partners are outdated as far as I'm concerned. What's important is that my choices don't hurt anyone."

2. "I take a hybrid position when it comes to the Bible's instructions on sexuality. Its teachings on monogamous, lifelong marriage are beautiful, and I believe sex within monogamous, lifelong marriage is ethical, whether heterosexual or homosexual."

3. "I believe the Bible consistently teaches that sex is ethical only within a lifelong marriage between a man and a woman. So, that's how I choose to live."

WHAT DO THE FOLLOWING SCRIPTURES TEACH YOU ABOUT SEXUALITY?

Matthew 5:27–31	
Ephesians 5:25–33	
1 Thessalonians 4:3–7	
1 Corinthians 6:9–20	

PICK A REAL-LIFE DILEMMA WHEN IT COMES TO SEXUALITY:

1. As I vote, should I care more about supporting policies which advance LGBTQ rights (e.g., polyamorous marriage, transgender sports, inclusive bathrooms) or about supporting policies which safeguard religious freedom (e.g., the rights of Christian pastors to preach culturally unpopular biblical truth about sexuality, the rights of Christian colleges to hold their faculty and students to biblical norms of sexuality)? *Romans 1:26–27; 1 Timothy 2:1–2.*

2. How would I respond to this argument for cohabitation (a couple living together sexually before marriage): "You wouldn't

buy a shoe without first trying it on"? *Hebrews 13:4; Matthew 19:4–6.*

3. If my friend invites me to their same-sex marriage, will I attend? *Romans 1:26–27; Matthew 19:4–6; Matthew 9:10–13.*

WHAT CHRISTLIKE CHARACTER TRAITS (VIRTUES AND VALUES) OUGHT TO INFORM YOUR RESPONSE TO THE DILEMMA? (FEEL FREE TO LOOK BACK AT CHAPTER 11 OR AHEAD AT APPENDIX A FOR A LIST OF JESUS' VALUES FROM THE GOSPEL OF MATTHEW.)

WHAT COMMANDS OF SCRIPTURE (DOS AND DON'TS) OUGHT TO INFORM YOUR RESPONSE TO THE DILEMMA?

WHAT CONSEQUENCES DO YOU INTEND TO HAPPEN (AND NOT HAPPEN) AS A RESULT OF YOUR DECISION/VIEW?

FILL IN THE BLANKS:

As a person of ___ (fill in with virtues) who values ___ (fill in with values),

I will obey ___ (fill in with commands)

by ___ (fill in with your decision/view)

in such a way that ___ (fill in with consequences).

14
WHAT DOES CHRISTIANITY TEACH ABOUT THE WOMB?

A few years ago, as I (Daniel) was driving through town, with the hospital on my right, I glanced over at the digital billboard screen outside the hospital. As usual, the screen was circulating through photos of newborn babies that had been born at the hospital that week. When I saw them this time, I was curious and got to thinking: Why was it the *baby* who was featured on the screen? It was not a picture of the mom who carried the baby before birth, or a picture of the doctor or the labor and delivery nurses who delivered the baby— yet these are the people who deserve credit for doing the work. Still, we all get it: it's the tiniest members of our community who deserve the biggest celebration, the cutest outfits, the most pictures, the most inflated compliments, the sweetest kisses, the heartiest welcomes. It's the littlest people who have the largest value. The most helpless among us are also our most precious.

How did we come to know that?

The world did not always think this way. The Greco-Roman world of the first century A.D. did not believe that the most helpless are the most precious.

Often, wealthy people did not want kids. To wealthy people without kids would flow a perpetual flattery of gifts, dinner invitations, and whatever else it took to get oneself included in the will. The childless rich were treated as royalty.[24] While childlessness sometimes meant luck, a woman discovering she was pregnant sometimes meant inconvenience. When undesired pregnancies occurred, a pregnant woman could ingest certain potions intended to abort the child, a practice encouraged by some of the era's greatest ethicists.[25] More frequent than abortion was the practice of "exposing" the child, dumping her or him, for example, outside of town.

Then Jesus came and began a movement that changed the way the world sees and values children. It was Jesus who taught his followers, "Let the little children come to me, and do not hinder them, for the kingdom of God belongs to such as these" (Mark 10:14). His followers challenged the world around them to stop treating children as discardable. One Christian named Tertullian asked his culture how is it that they could throw their babies out into "cold, starvation, and [to be eaten by] the dogs." Another Christian named Clement tried to get his culture to see their grotesque value system: they had tons of money, yet they threw away their babies while keeping exotic pets.[26]

The Christians' advocacy exceeded talk. With the average life expectancy of the era being 30

THE CHRISTIANS' ADVOCACY EXCEEDED TALK.

---

[24] Alvin J. Schmidt, *How Christianity Changed the World* (Grand Rapids: Zondervan, 2004), 55.
[25] Schmidt, 55–56.
[26] Albert A. Bell, Jr., *Exploring the New Testament World: An Illustrated Guide to the World of Jesus and the First Christians* (Nashville: Thomas Nelson, 1998), 241.

years old, the empire was overrun with orphans. From early on, it was Christians who took up offerings to take care of these orphans. Often, the Christians would rescue exposed babies and bring orphans in to live with their families. In the 300s, once Christianity was made legal, the church had the funds to begin building orphanages, often connected to their cathedrals.[27] Moreover, church leaders protested abortion and organized support for women with unwanted pregnancies. Eventually, their ethical positions were able to convince those at the empire's helm and, by A.D. 374, abortion, infanticide, and child exposing were all illegal.[28]

Let's walk through the following steps in order to respond to real-life dilemmas related to the womb.

WHICH OPTION DO YOU TEND TO CHOOSE WHEN IT COMES TO THE WOMB?

1. "Women should be free to do what they feel is necessary with their own bodies. It's a massive invasion of privacy and reproductive rights for the state to intrude on a women's right to choose abortion."

2. "It is difficult to say when the fetus gains personhood. This is why the state needs to be free to impose restrictions on abortion further along in the pregnancy process."

3. "A preborn baby is a human life from the moment of conception (what gets added after conception are things like food and water, not chromosomes). So, abortion (and birth control methods that cause abortion) kills a human life.

---

[27] Schmidt, 131–132.
[28] Schmidt, 59.

Any line we draw after conception at which the human life deserves protection from death (such as when the fetus gains self-awareness) is arbitrary and sets a dangerous precedent for people both unborn and born."

WHAT DO THE FOLLOWING SCRIPTURES TEACH YOU ABOUT THE WOMB?

Mark 10:13–16	
Proverbs 31:8–9	
Genesis 25:22; Luke 1:44; Psalm 139:13–15	
Genesis 1:26–28	

PICK A REAL-LIFE DILEMMA WHEN IT COMES TO THE WOMB:

(Because each of these three scenarios deal with the same issue from different angles, we are not giving specific scriptures for each; rather, we encourage you to look again at the scriptures above to form your thinking.)

1. If choosing a method of birth control for myself or my spouse, would I take the time to research which birth control methods are abortifacient (i.e., could cause abortions) and/or might treat embryos inhumanely?

2. How would I respond to the political argument that it's okay for a politician to be personally opposed to abortion but that they don't feel right imposing that personal conviction on others (e.g., through legislation)?

3. Is abortion an ethical option if it seems to be in the best interest of the mother's health (e.g., cancer medication which would help the mother but kill the unborn baby).

WHAT CHRISTLIKE CHARACTER TRAITS (VIRTUES AND VALUES) OUGHT TO INFORM YOUR RESPONSE TO THE DILEMMA? (FEEL FREE TO LOOK BACK AT CHAPTER 11 OR AHEAD AT APPENDIX A FOR A LIST OF JESUS' VALUES FROM THE GOSPEL OF MATTHEW.)

WHAT COMMANDS OF SCRIPTURE (DOS AND DON'TS) OUGHT TO INFORM YOUR RESPONSE TO THE DILEMMA?

WHAT CONSEQUENCES DO YOU INTEND TO HAPPEN (AND NOT HAPPEN) AS A RESULT OF YOUR DECISION/VIEW?

FILL IN THE BLANKS:

As a person of ____ (fill in with virtues) who values ____ (fill in with values),

I will obey ____ (fill in with commands)

by ____ (fill in with your decision/view)

in such a way that ____ (fill in with consequences).

15
WHAT DOES CHRISTIANITY TEACH ABOUT THE DEATHBED?

When a person says, "This is a matter life or death," the statement is meant to impart a sense of urgency (i.e., we've got to do something *now*) and clarity (i.e., this is not a hard decision).

The problem is, when it comes to ethical issues of life and death, many of these have become very confusing. We're referring to ethical issues such as physician-assisted suicide, euthanasia, and capital punishment. Jack Kevorkian was once known as "Dr. Death"—a villainous physician who assisted people in their suicides and was eventually jailed for it. Yet, it's not hard to find influential voices which now paint Kevorkian as more of a pioneer than villain. Which is it?

To make matters muddier, many who champion our "right to die"—because it should be our decision, our freedom—ignore that historically we see a slippery slope from "right to die" to *duty* to die. The reasoning behind this change goes something like this: "After all,

IT'S A SLIPPERY SLOPE FROM "RIGHT TO DIE" TO DUTY TO DIE.

you're taking up a lot of resources, and we're planning to stop paying for such-and-such anyway. And you don't want to be a burden to your family anymore, do you?"

Then there's the issue of capital punishment. No controversy or confusion there, right? Actually, a lot of the population thinks it can be morally permissible to kill an unborn, "unwanted" baby, yet morally unthinkable to kill a convicted murderer and rapist. On the other hand, isn't capital punishment clearly permitted in the Bible? It is (see Genesis 9:6), but then again, the biblical criteria for putting someone to death is that it's got to be on the basis of two or three eyewitnesses (Deuteronomy 17:6), and it's hardly ever the case that people on death row today are able to be convicted on that strict a standard.

Let's walk through the following steps in order to respond to real-life dilemmas related to the deathbed.

WHICH OPTION DO YOU TEND TO CHOOSE WHEN IT COMES TO THE DEATHBED?

Physician-assisted suicide:

1. "I value compassion for the sufferer more than strict adherence to an ethic that not everybody accepts. Assisted suicide ought to be legal."

2. "I can support comfort measures (e.g., shifting the focus to easing pain when life-prolonging measures are no longer a working option) but never assisted suicide."

Capital punishment (death penalty):

1. "Capital punishment is wrong in principle because it is the taking of human life."

FOLLOWING JESUS IN A POLITICALLY DIVIDED WORLD

2. "Capital punishment might be right in principle, but because we have trouble knowing if someone is guilty for sure and because we have trouble being fair in carrying it out (e.g., when it depends on who can afford better lawyers), we ought to prohibit capital punishment in practice."

3. "Capital punishment has biblical warrant, and when carried out consistently, it is a strong deterrent to the worst crimes."

WHAT DO THE FOLLOWING SCRIPTURES TEACH YOU ABOUT THE DEATHBED?

1 Kings 19:1–18	
2 Corinthians 1:8–11	
Genesis 9:6; Romans 13:4	
Numbers 35:30	

PICK A REAL-LIFE DILEMMA WHEN IT COMES TO THE DEATHBED:

1. Would I support the legality of physician-assisted suicide in my region? *1 Corinthians 15:26; Exodus 20:13.*

120

2. Let's say that most people around me are making a consequence-based argument about capital punishment (e.g., it is good because it deters crime; or, it is bad because it leads to wrongful, irreversible convictions). As a Christian, how can I deepen the conversation by taking a position based on more than just consequences? *Genesis 9:6; Romans 13:4; Numbers 35:30.*

3. If I were feeling suicidal, how would I respond to my suicidal thoughts as a disciple of Jesus? *Philippians 4:8–9; 1 Peter 5:6–7; Psalm 42:5.*

WHAT CHRISTLIKE CHARACTER TRAITS (VIRTUES AND VALUES) OUGHT TO INFORM YOUR RESPONSE TO THE DILEMMA? (FEEL FREE TO LOOK BACK AT CHAPTER 11 OR AHEAD AT APPENDIX A FOR A LIST OF JESUS' VALUES FROM THE GOSPEL OF MATTHEW.)

WHAT COMMANDS OF SCRIPTURE (DOS AND DON'TS) OUGHT TO INFORM YOUR RESPONSE TO THE DILEMMA?

WHAT CONSEQUENCES DO YOU INTEND TO HAPPEN (AND NOT HAPPEN) AS A RESULT OF YOUR DECISION/VIEW?

FILL IN THE BLANKS:

As a person of ___ (fill in with virtues) who values ___ (fill in with values),

I will obey ___ (fill in with commands)

by ___ (fill in with your decision/view)

in such a way that ___ (fill in with consequences).

16
WHAT DOES CHRISTIANITY TEACH ABOUT THE ENVIRONMENT?

Isn't a chapter on Christianity and the environment taking us a bit out of our lane? Does the Bible have anything helpful to add to the conversation about whether plastic is worth recycling or McDonald's burgers are okay to eat?

Clearly, one way Christianity applies to the conversation is by reminding us we're not supposed to kill each other. There's often a bitter impasse between, on the one hand, those who believe humans are guilty of animal abuse/genocide, planetary destruction, and treating our land, sea, and atmosphere as garbage dumps, and, on the other hand, those who are weary of the apocalyptic fears, economic disruption, and human guilt that come along with many environmental proposals.

A core disagreement comes down to whether we should prioritize environmental or economic concerns: is it better to concern yourself with the planet's environmental needs or with your organization's financial needs? There are no quick, easy answers here, but into the dilemma the Bible offers crucial truth about who we are as humans and why God placed us here.

In the Bible's first chapter, God is at work creating and filling the heavens and the earth. In Genesis chapter 1, after God creates parts of our universe, the refrain is always the same: "God saw that it was good" (Genesis 1:4, 12, 18, 21, 25). Then God stepped back and "saw all that he had made, and it was very good" (Genesis 1:31). God and his Son continue to work today (John 5:17), and reflective people continue to marvel at their works (Psalm 8:3). After putting the finishing touches on his creation in Genesis 1, in the next chapter, God places his human image bearers into a garden he created, telling them to "work it and take care of it" (Genesis 2:15).

Christianity teaches that our specialness as a species is exactly why we are given the job of tending the rest of God's creation. Seeing environmental needs around us is not a cue to minimize the role humans are to play, but rather to underscore it. Human work, far from being exploitative of its environmental context, is meant to have that context in its scope.

Yet, even before we leave the first book of the Bible, we see heartbreaking examples of work turning dark. We see prostitution becoming a cultural norm (see Genesis 38). We see a shrewd uncle taking advantage of his nephew's work (Genesis 29–31). We see a young man sold into slavery by his jealous brothers (Genesis 37) and the slave taken advantage of through deception and neglect (Genesis 39–40). By the beginning of Exodus, an entire people group has become another people's slaves.

Because of this tendency toward corruption and exploitation, the Jewish law puts into place various commands; for example, they were forbidden from holding back wages overnight (Leviticus 19:13), taking advantage of a poor hired worker (Deuteronomy 24:14), or keeping Israelite slaves except as hired workers (Leviticus 25:39–43). These concerns expand to the land and animals , as well (e.g., Leviticus 25:1–7; Deuteronomy 22:10; 25:4).

> **THESE CONCERNS EXPAND TO THE LAND AND ANIMALS.**

The Bible doesn't answer whether it's more accurate to use the term "climate crisis" or "climate hysteria." It doesn't tell us whether ecological concerns are better met through a carefully regulated society or a profitable society able to devote greater attention to its environment. But the Bible clearly sets before us a noble task God gave us at our beginning and continues to move us toward as his children and stewards of his creation:

> "For the creation was subjected to frustration, not by its own choice, but by the will of the one who subjected it, in hope that the creation itself will be liberated from its bondage to decay and brought into the freedom and glory of the children of God." (Romans 8:20–21)

In the words of New Testament theologian Matthew Bates, "Transformed disciples make God's new-creation glory present in the world."[29]

---

[29] Matthew W. Bates, *The Gospel Precisely: Surprisingly Good News About Jesus Christ the King* (Renew.org, 2021), 68.

WHICH OPTION DO YOU TEND TO CHOOSE WHEN IT COMES TO THE ENVIRONMENT?

1. "In the grand scheme of things, Christians honestly shouldn't care about what happens to the wider environment. In the end, it will all burn, anyway."

2. "If life weren't so demanding, I might care more about addressing environmental problems such as pollution or animal abuse. As it stands, it's extremely low on my list of priorities."

3. "As a Christian, I include environmental concerns as part of how I try to follow Jesus in every area of life."

4. "For me, environmental crises (e.g., climate change) and environmental crimes (e.g., fast-food industry) take first place in terms of urgency and priority."

WHAT DO THE FOLLOWING SCRIPTURES TEACH YOU ABOUT THE ENVIRONMENT?

Psalm 115:16	
Psalm 8:3–8	
Genesis 1:26–31	
Leviticus 25:1–7; Deuteronomy 22:10; 25:4	

PICK A REAL-LIFE DILEMMA WHEN IT COMES TO THE ENVIRONMENT:

1. What steps can I take to help me distinguish between environmental hype meant to control me and legitimate environmental concerns that should influence how I live and vote? *Proverbs 18:17; Matthew 12:11–12; James 4:17.*

2. How can I work hard and make money without succumbing to the sins of greed and exploitation? *Ephesians 4:28; James 5:1–6; 1 Timothy 6:6–10.*

3. As a Christian, is it okay for me to eat meat? *Genesis 1:29; John 21:7–13; Acts 11:5–10.*

WHAT CHRISTLIKE CHARACTER TRAITS (VIRTUES AND VALUES) OUGHT TO INFORM YOUR RESPONSE TO THE DILEMMA? (FEEL FREE TO LOOK BACK AT CHAPTER 11 OR AHEAD AT APPENDIX A FOR A LIST OF JESUS' VALUES FROM THE GOSPEL OF MATTHEW.)

WHAT COMMANDS OF SCRIPTURE (DOS AND DON'TS) OUGHT TO INFORM YOUR RESPONSE TO THE DILEMMA?

WHAT CONSEQUENCES DO YOU INTEND TO HAPPEN (AND NOT HAPPEN) AS A RESULT OF YOUR DECISION/VIEW?

FILL IN THE BLANKS:

As a person of ____ (fill in with virtues) who values ____ (fill in with values),

I will obey ____ (fill in with commands)

by ____ (fill in with your decision/view)

in such a way that ____ (fill in with consequences).

17
WHAT DOES CHRISTIANITY TEACH ABOUT THE DISADVANTAGED?

Throughout the Bible, God shows and tells how he cares about lifting up the poor and oppressed. When the Jews had suffered in slavery under the Egyptians, God's compassion was awakened. In the Exodus, he rescued the Jews while plaguing and impoverishing the Egyptians in a grand reversal of fortunes.

After Israel was established as a nation, God sent them prophets to remind Israel that God has a heart for the poor. For example, in the prophet Micah's writings, we learn that, though God's people were busily offering sacrifices to God in their temple, they were mistreating the poor through dishonest scales and violence. This provoked God to give the following message through Micah: "He has shown you, O mortal, what is good. And what does the Lord require of you? To act justly and to love mercy and to walk humbly with your God" (Micah 6:8). To summarize, they were not treating the poor fairly, and they needed to act justly toward them.

In the New Testament, Jesus described his mission as a mission of liberation, and his compassionate words and actions showed he wasn't just referring to a mystical type of spiritual liberation:

"The Spirit of the Lord is on me, because he has anointed me to proclaim good news to the poor. He has sent me

> ## HE HAS ANOINTED ME TO PROCLAIM GOOD NEWS TO THE POOR.

to proclaim freedom for the prisoners and recovery of sight for the blind, to set the oppressed free, to proclaim the year of the Lord's favor." (Luke 4:18–19)

Does God care about helping people living in oppression and poverty? The answer should be uncontroversial. Yet *how* we help the poor and oppressed in our own time is a matter of great complication and controversy. Are people in poverty lifted out of it by more governmental intervention or less? Are porous national borders ultimately a good thing (e.g., they help the foreigner in need) or a bad thing (e.g., they make the nation less secure)? Is "gender-affirming care" for the trans minor something that will ultimately save—or damage—their lives?

Let's walk through the following steps in order to respond to real-life dilemmas related to the disadvantaged.

WHICH OPTION DO YOU TEND TO CHOOSE WHEN IT COMES TO THE DISADVANTAGED?

1. "In a perfect world, I might be able to consider other people's needs, but life is hard enough just getting through and providing for my own family."

2. "I want to belong to a church that radically recenters its priorities around the needs of the disadvantaged, such that they publicly support policies which center on the disadvantaged (e.g., increased decriminalization of drugs, redistribution of wealth) and they reinterpret biblical texts in ways that center disadvantaged voices (e.g., pro-gay theology)."

3. "I want to help disadvantaged people in ways that flow from a worldview grounded in God and his truth. The gospel is first and foremost about King Jesus, risen and reigning and coming again. I can help disadvantaged people best by serving them in Jesus' name and pointing them to bow their knee to Jesus, who invites them into life as they were meant to live it."

WHAT DO THE FOLLOWING SCRIPTURES TEACH YOU ABOUT THE DISADVANTAGED?

Matthew 25:31–40	
James 2:1–7	
Acts 2:43–47	
Exodus 22:21–23	

PICK A REAL-LIFE DILEMMA WHEN IT COMES TO THE DISADVANTAGED:

1. What factors will help me decide what types of charity work I will personally support? *2 Corinthians 8:1–6; 8:16–21.*

2. Let's say I am friends with a fellow Christian who is resentful and angry toward undocumented immigrants coming into the country. My friend has no political/law enforcement ability to secure the border, and they are unable to do anything about it except grow in anger and anxiety. What's my advice for my friend? *Luke 10:25–37; Ephesians 4:26–27.*

3. Is it better to vote for free-market politicians that incentivize hard work and economic achievement (with the added risk that

there will be financial losers) or more progressive politicians that support policies centered on the poor, such as a universal basic income and raised minimum wage (with the added risk that they are incentivizing victimhood)? *2 Thessalonians 3:6–10; James 1:27; Deuteronomy 15:11.*

WHAT CHRISTLIKE CHARACTER TRAITS (VIRTUES AND VALUES) OUGHT TO INFORM YOUR RESPONSE TO THE DILEMMA? (FEEL FREE TO LOOK BACK AT CHAPTER 11 OR AHEAD AT APPENDIX A FOR A LIST OF JESUS' VALUES FROM THE GOSPEL OF MATTHEW.)

WHAT COMMANDS OF SCRIPTURE (DOS AND DON'TS) OUGHT TO INFORM YOUR RESPONSE TO THE DILEMMA?

WHAT CONSEQUENCES DO YOU INTEND TO HAPPEN (AND NOT HAPPEN) AS A RESULT OF YOUR DECISION/VIEW?

FILL IN THE BLANKS:

As a person of ___ (fill in with virtues) who values ___ (fill in with values),

I will obey ___ (fill in with commands)

by ___ (fill in with your decision/view)

in such a way that ___ (fill in with consequences).

18
WHAT DOES CHRISTIANITY TEACH ABOUT THE BATTLEFIELD?

War.

Is it ever good? Is it a necessary evil, or an absolute evil? Is participation in war an unacceptable compromise for Christians, or simply a way for Christians to be good citizens of the nation in which God has placed them?

War is one of those issues that can deeply divide the church. On one end of the spectrum, you can find a "God wills it" attitude. In A.D. 1095, Pope Urban II preached a sermon proclaiming a crusade to take back the Holy Land, so that pilgrims would no longer be threatened on their pilgrimages. If you went on the crusade, the Pope promised, you would be forgiven of past sins, and you would have the rights to the land that you took. At the end of the Pope's sermon, a roar arose from the crowd: "God wills it! God wills it!"

On the other end of the spectrum, you have complete and unconditional nonviolence as the only way for the people of Jesus. On this end, you'll hear Christians say that Dietrich Bonhoeffer's participation in the plot to kill Hitler was a betrayal of the gospel. According to this view, to be a Christian is to be devoted to nonviolence at all times and in all cases. Participation in war is out.

When the Beatles' front man John Lennon wrote about war, he said that in order to have peace, we need to get rid of countries. And the ideas of heaven and hell. And religion. "Imagine there's no countries," he sang, "It isn't hard to do. Nothing to kill or die for—and no religion too. Imagine all the people living life in peace. You may say I'm a dreamer, but I'm not the only one. I hope someday you'll join us, and the world will be as one."[30]

John Lennon saw people passionately believing their religious beliefs, and he apparently thought to himself, "I think that's the problem."

Let's live in such a way that people see the way we passionately hold our religious convictions, and think to themselves, "I think that's the solution."

How? For one thing, we can start by holding our convictions with love toward each other. John 13:35 says, "By this everyone will know that you are my disciples, if you love one another." A Christian for whom nonviolence is always a **BY THIS EVERYONE WILL KNOW THAT YOU ARE MY DISCIPLES.** nonnegotiable can still extend graciousness to the Christian in active military, noting that, when soldiers came to John the Baptist in repentance, he did not tell them to leave their post, but rather not to use their position for selfish gain (Luke 3:14). In the same way, the patriotic Christian for whom the U.S. military has been effective

---

[30] John Lennon, Lyrics to "Imagine." Performed by John Lennon, Ascot Sound Studios, 1971, *Genius*, https://genius.com/John-lennon-imagine-lyrics.

at keeping evil at bay can still show gentleness toward the Christian who can't square Jesus' teachings on "turning the other cheek" with military participation.

As followers of Jesus, we can start being perceived by the surrounding culture as having the solution when we refuse to be warlike toward each other when we disagree.

Let's walk through the following steps in order to respond to real-life dilemmas related to the battlefield.

WHICH OPTION DO YOU TEND TO CHOOSE WHEN IT COMES TO THE BATTLEFIELD?

1. "As a person of nonviolence, I do not advocate Christians participating in the military, even in a noncombative role."

2. "As a person of nonviolence, I do not advocate Christians participating in a combative role in the military, although it would not be wrong to participate in a noncombative role."

3. "I believe it is permissible for a Christian to be involved in war, as long as it is a just war (e.g., the reason for war is unprovoked aggression, diplomatic means are unsuccessful, the objectives of the war are limited, etc.)."

4. "I believe that not only are wars sometimes just, but that sometimes preventive strikes are necessary (that is, sometimes the military needs to be the aggressor in order to bring about a better outcome in the end)."

WHAT DO THE FOLLOWING SCRIPTURES TEACH YOU ABOUT THE BATTLEFIELD?

Isaiah 2:3–5; Psalm 46:8–10	
Matthew 5:9	
Matthew 5:38–48	
Romans 13:1–7	

PICK A REAL-LIFE DILEMMA WHEN IT COMES TO THE BATTLEFIELD:

1. Can I participate in active military as a disciple of Jesus? *Luke 3:14; Luke 6:27–31.*

2. At what points will I no longer be able to agree with my country as to what counts as a just war? What lines would need to be crossed? *Amos 1:3–15; Jeremiah 22:3.*

3. If nonviolence is a major part of my ethic as a Christian, do I think that it also ought to be applied to the state (e.g., the military, the police)? And, if the answer is yes, how might I propose the state keep peace, without the threat of force? *1 Peter 2:13–14; Romans 13:1–7.*

WHAT CHRISTLIKE CHARACTER TRAITS (VIRTUES AND VALUES) OUGHT TO INFORM YOUR RESPONSE TO THE DILEMMA? (FEEL FREE TO LOOK BACK AT CHAPTER 11 OR AHEAD AT APPENDIX A FOR A LIST OF JESUS' VALUES FROM THE GOSPEL OF MATTHEW.)

WHAT COMMANDS OF SCRIPTURE (DOS AND DON'TS) OUGHT TO INFORM YOUR RESPONSE TO THE DILEMMA?

WHAT CONSEQUENCES DO YOU INTEND TO HAPPEN (AND NOT HAPPEN) AS A RESULT OF YOUR DECISION/VIEW?

FILL IN THE BLANKS:

As a person of ___ (fill in with virtues) who values ___ (fill in with values),

I will obey ___ (fill in with commands)

by ___ (fill in with your decision/view)

in such a way that ___ (fill in with consequences).

Before continuing with the final few chapters of this book, let's pause for a moment to reflect on what the previous seven chapters have provided. In addition to helping you think through specific scenarios within those seven topics, we've also aimed to provide you with a process you can apply to additional issues that are important to the political conversation. You can use that same process to deepen and sharpen your thinking on topics such as:

- Surveillance
- Education
- Parental rights
- Generative artificial intelligence
- LGBTQ issues
- Globalism VS nationalism
- The economy
- Censorship

And obviously any other relevant topic.

So, our hope is that you will mark this section of the book so that you can come back here to review the process and apply to a new scenario when one comes up. Again, the aim is that as followers of Jesus, our thinking about such issues will be shaped by our Christian character and rooted in the commands of Scripture so that our political convictions and behavior honor King Jesus.

PART 3 - QUESTIONS TO FUEL CREATIVITY & COURAGE

19
WHAT IS BETTER THAN CRITICIZING THE CULTURE?

Fact: it's easier to criticize "them"—those people out there—than to do the hard work needed to offer something better.

Posting mocking memes.

Ridiculing on Reels.

Using spiteful or derogatory rhetoric in conversation.

That's easy.

But the early Christians model a better, more powerful path. Surrounded as they were by the abyss of Roman pagan culture,

> **THE EARLY CHRISTIANS MODEL A BETTER, MORE POWERFUL PATH.**

the early Christians offered people a better way of life. With no political power to post, picket, or protest, they transformed the world by presenting and calling people into an alternative culture, something radically different than what was all around them.

A beautiful description of this can be found in chapter 39 of Tertullian's *Apology.*[31] Having spent earlier chapters defending the

---

[31] Tertullian, Chapter 39, Apology, New Advent, https://www.newadvent.org/fathers/0301.htm.

Christians against the evils of which they were accused, Tertullian then turns in chapter 39 to the positive good found in the church. The church does not practice violence, Tertullian says, other than that they wrestle with God in prayer for the welfare of rulers, leaders, and all people in general. Christian leaders, he contends, obtain their position only on the basis of tried-and-true character. They collect offerings (which are purely voluntary) not to spend on things they enjoy, but to care for the poor among them, to provide for the needs of children, or to look after the aged and those imprisoned and exiled for their faith.

Indeed, Tertullian claims that what brands the Christians is their noble love for one another (so much so that their pagan neighbors exclaim, "see how they love one another!"). It's a love which stands in stark contrast to the hatred found in their culture at large.

In other words, the early Christians might not have been able to stop slander against them from the Empire as a whole, but they could and did impress those who actually knew them with their love and manner of life.

This is far greater than criticizing culture for all its shortcomings and sins.

So, in view of our calling to be an outpost of heaven in our community, we ought to work hard at forming and offering a better culture. An alternative culture. A culture that will "adorn the doctrine of God" (Titus 2:10, NASB).

This is what Jesus means when he describes his followers as salt and light in Matthew 5:13–16. Jesus states this as a matter of fact. This is who we are in the world. We *are* salt. We *are* light. How do we live this out? In my (John's) early years, this conviction was always associated with personal evangelism. Be salt and light by sharing the gospel. While that's good, that's not what Jesus says. He says we live out our identity as salt and light by shining forth "our good works" in such a way that people glorify our Father in heaven (Matthew 5:16).

And what good works does he have in mind? The kind of things taught in the rest of the Sermon on the Mount. Operating without anger and contempt. Eliminating lust. Practicing marital fidelity. Acting with complete integrity. Loving our enemies. And all the other things Jesus instructs us to do now that we've entered his kingdom.

Now certainly, as Jesus notes, we can lose our saltiness and we can hide our light. How would we do that? Once again, I was taught that this meant *not sharing the gospel,* and that's not unimportant to recognize. But once we see what Jesus is talking about, it becomes clear that we lose our saltiness and hide our light by failing to live out the good life that Jesus calls us into and intends to form among us.

So just imagine with us for a moment . . . what would it be like if we[32] actually lived out the Sermon on the Mount (as well as other instructions by Jesus and his apostles)?

Imagine…

• a community marked with patience and peace rather than anger and contempt, where anger is no longer seen as necessary for getting your way or protecting your interests and where name-calling and labeling is rejected in favor of reconciliation and harmony.

---

[32] The plural is important. Jesus describes it as a *city* on a hill, and a city entails a group of people. So, it's we, not just me—an alternative city that presents a beautifully good way of being human.

• a people who reject not only adultery but also the ensnaring sexual desires outside of God's boundaries that cause it and so many other sexual evils . . . a people who do not carry out sexual harassment, or sexual abuse, or any other harmful sexual activity, but instead are personally committed to sexual purity and faithfulness.

• marriages which routinely last a lifetime because the people in them have character marked by faithfulness and self-giving love, which make this possible.

• a people who are known to be completely trustworthy because they act with genuine integrity and their word is their bond.

• humans who are actively kind, even toward those who hurt them or oppose them; they freely share their possessions and do good to all people, even actively doing deeds of love for their enemies.

• a people of faith but whose piety goes beyond merely keeping up religious appearances and who actually seek to be genuinely good; people who regularly and sincerely treat other people the way they themselves want to be treated.

Can you imagine? It almost sounds too good to be true, doesn't it?

That's the kingdom vision of Jesus in the Sermon on the Mount. If we are going to be a holy nation and a royal priesthood, this is the kind of people we must become. It's in this way that we live as salt that hasn't lost its saltiness and as light that isn't hidden it under a basket. Living this way, we exist *for* the world by providing a concrete model of human flourishing and offering an alternative society that attracts people to God's truth.

And this is how the church once transformed the world.

Not by living this way perfectly, of course. In fact, Jesus has instructions for us when we fail to live this way. But even though the early Christians did not live it perfectly, they did believe living this way was possible and sought to embody it genuinely and substantially. Doing this is much more powerful than expecting a fallen world to live up to Christian values and virtues, and then harshly criticizing people when they don't—especially when we ourselves are not living up to these values and virtues very well, either.

So, a question for you . . . actually, a series of questions.

What if our churches became greenhouses for human flourishing?

What if instead of standing on the sidelines of human goodness, criticizing and mocking, we entered into the fray of becoming genuinely good human beings who embody the character of Christ by grace and by the Spirit?

What if we became so conformed to the image of Christ that we demonstrated love and did good for the righteous and unrighteous alike (Matthew 5:43–48)?

What if, like the Christians of Tertullian's day, we were known by our genuine and great love for one another and for all people?

A disciple of Jesus goes beyond criticizing what's wrong in the culture by creating culture in which Jesus is King.

ACTION STEPS

1. Romans 12:9–21 describes some ways disciples of Jesus can "overcome evil with good." Reflect on and write down a few specific examples of how you can overcome evil with good toward both believers (who may disagree with you) and unbelievers in your spheres of influence—at home, in your neighborhood, among your coworkers, at your school, etc.

20
WHAT ARE YOU DISCIPLING PEOPLE TO BE?

When it comes to politics, many people in the U.S. have arrived at the place where they feel your politics no longer tell them just your vision for the country. Your politics also tell them whether or not you're a good person. They might think, *Can such-and-such even call himself Christian when he doesn't vote like I do?* In a post-Christian world, politics itself too often becomes the new religion that one adheres to, with all the idols that come along with it.

So, how do we seek to make disciples who don't bow to political idols, on either the right or the left? Here are three things to remember as you are discipling people.

YOU'RE NOT DISCIPLING PEOPLE TO BE MILITANTS.

When we say "militants," we mean politically aggressive, politically pugnacious—ever ready for a political debate where they can own the liberal or destroy the conservative.

There isn't a definitive Christian view on every single political position. And even when there is a Christian view, we need to hold that view with a posture of kindness and understanding. Nobody is drawn to Jesus through pugnacious social media debates or through red faces and raised voices at family dinners.

> **NOBODY IS DRAWN TO JESUS THROUGH PUGNACIOUS SOCIAL MEDIA DEBATES.**

One of the most important questions facing our churches now and in the coming years is this: *what exactly is our fight?* There will never be a shortage of issues to fight about. And if the past few years in the U.S. have taught us anything about our churches, it's that Bible-believing churches can still get mixed up about what battle they signed up for. Masks. Trump. Vaccines. You may have wounds from 2020 that still haven't closed up yet. You might have friendships that died in one of the battles in the War of 2020.

We need to remember that there were a lot of battles that Jesus simply said *no* to. They weren't his thing. For example, once when two brothers were fighting over their inheritance, one brother asked Jesus to intervene. Jesus told him it wasn't his fight: "Man, who appointed me a judge or an arbiter between?" (Luke 12:14). He sent the man on his way with a warning to stay away from greed.

At the time, there was a theology argument about the right place to worship. The Jews believed it was in Judea, and the Samaritans believed it was in Samaria. Jesus told the Samaritan who brought it up that the location was not what matters. What matters, he told her, is that she was spiritually parched, and he could give her living, lasting water (John 4:4–26).

Another example of this was when Peter fought Jesus' arrest. Peter got one good slice in—one ear—when Jesus told him to stop, saying essentially that this was not their fight.

We're not discipling people to be militants. So, sometimes it's okay to say *no* to a political fight. That's one way we can help disciple people not to bow to idols on the right or the left: we can remember we're not discipling people to become aggressors who are eager to jump into a political fight.

YOU'RE NOT DISCIPLING PEOPLE TO BE MERCENARIES.

Sometimes there are battles that *are* worth fighting. There are ethical questions that have become political which you do need to engage because that's a way to stay faithful to God's truth and to love your neighbor.

However, this is where you need to remember that we're not discipling people to be mercenaries. Mercenaries are soldiers from one country who sign on to fight for another country. When you do engage in politics, as a Christian, you've got to be careful that you don't get conscripted into someone else's kingdom, someone else's army. Put simply, you're not discipling people to be Republicans or Democrats. That's not to say there's a moral equivalence between the two political platforms; it is to say that the goal of Christian discipleship is far deeper and more nuanced than point-by-point alignment with a political party.

If we're not careful and we engage politically without thinking critically, we can end up worshiping Jesus tepidly while engaging the issues wholeheartedly. We will be less discipling people and more fattening them up into a juicy voting bloc. When we "believe" Jesus somewhere in the back of our minds but we *feel* our politics in our bones, we're going to disciple people to be less citizens of Jesus' kingdom and more mercenaries to a partisan platform.

You can be a part of Jesus' kingdom in theory, but your compassion for the poor is actually being coopted by the political left, so that you're taking your cues about justice more from secular progressivism than from Jesus. Or your concern for moral order and for religious freedom as a Christian could be coopted by the political right, so that you begin to value the Christian faith most of all for how it helps build a strong country.

How do you know when you're becoming more a mercenary of the right or left than a citizen of King Jesus? Well, you become one hand clapping. You starting seeing that one political party as always wrong and the people on that side are "idiots" worthy of nothing but contempt.

When you make disciples, you're not discipling them to be militants or mercenaries. So, what are you discipling people to be?

> **YOU'RE NOT DISCIPLING THEM TO BE MILITANTS OR MERCENARIES.**

YOU ARE DISCIPLING PEOPLE TO BE MISSIONARIES.

Cross-cultural missionaries are often the best positioned to realize that God loves *all* people. When God sent Peter to a Roman centurion's house to tell him about Jesus, Peter said, "Truly I understand that God shows no partiality, but in every nation anyone who fears him and does what is right is acceptable to him" (Acts 10:34–35).

One of the most missions-minded churches I (Daniel) am aware of (where they're giving over 50% of their income to missions) has their atrium decorated with flags from nations all around the world. They're equipping it to look like heaven, where we will be among "a great multitude that no one could number, from every nation, from all tribes and peoples and languages, standing before the throne and before the Lamb" (Revelation 7:9).

Imagine that you are a missionary to another country. As a missionary, you would now be considered a foreigner among the nationals, and you would seek to find things to appreciate about the national culture, even if it was sometimes difficult for you. You would remind yourself that God loves all people—and that the nation you have moved *to* is just as important to God as the nation you have moved *from*.

Are you able to imagine yourself as a missionary to another nation? Good. Then give your imagination another challenge: imagine yourself as a missionary *here*.

If you were living as a missionary here in America (or substitute whatever country is your homeland), you would try to love the people as they are. You would find things in the culture to genuinely compliment, even as you noticed things that irked you. This is similar to the apostle Paul in Athens, so discouraged and disturbed by the idols he saw everywhere, and yet, when he had an opportunity to talk to the Athenians, he started by saying what? "People of Athens! I see that in every way you are very religious" (Acts 17:22).

As a missionary to this country, you would find common ground for building bridges to Jesus. Maybe it would be, "I sure appreciate how you care about welcoming marginalized people." Or,

"I sure appreciate how you care about building strong families." You would find bridges for pointing people to Jesus—who transforms civilizations not by starting with legislation, but by starting with the *inner life* of regular people.

As a missionary, you would resist any urge to demonize or canonize the people that are respected there. Whichever political side you aligned with, as a missionary, you would try to find things in the "other" America which you could value. You would need to discern the hopes and dreams of the other side which you can use to build bridges to the gospel.

For example, as a missionary to America, even if you are troubled by Californian politics, you would not joke about hoping that California falls into the sea. Or, as a missionary to America, if you lean toward blue-state politics, it would still be off-limits to denigrate the red states as "ignorant hicks." We want to live by the conviction that we have one King, and he teaches us to love all people of all nations, even our own.

> **WE WANT TO LIVE BY THE CONVICTION THAT WE HAVE ONE KING.**

Thinking like a missionary will help you guard against the extremes of unfair anti-Americanism as well as unquestioning nationalism. Thinking like a missionary can help you have better family get-togethers. Thinking like a missionary can help you keep your church from dividing. Most importantly, thinking like a missionary will likely mean more people in heaven.

So, how do we disciple people who do not bow to idols on the right or the left? By remembering that we're discipling people not to be militants or mercenaries, but to be missionaries.

RAISING JOEY AND ZOË

Let's say you have two children, Joey and Zoë. Joey has a high sense of moral standards, and Zoë has a bleeding-heart level of empathy. They're both school-aged and have been exposed to the rainbow flags around town and the pride shows on Disney+. They both have friends who have started identifying as transgender and as fairies and as furries, etc.

Let's say that Joey tends to see people as either *good* or *bad*, and he has the sense that LGBTQ+ people are bad people doing bad things and messing up our world. On the other hand, Zoë tends to see people not so much as good or bad, but as privileged or oppressed. Since people in LGBTQ+ communities have historically been oppressed and marginalized, she has a lot of empathy for them and tends to agree with them on what's right and wrong.

So, which kid is correct? If you trace the trajectory they are on, Zoë may end up being the person described at the end of Romans 1, applauding evil things. Joey may end up a Pharisee, where he sees you as either a good person (like him) or a bad person.

What both kids need is the gospel of King Jesus who brought a kingdom of grace and truth. In his kingdom, King Jesus brings together Pharisees and tax collectors to the same table under his lordship. In Jesus' kingdom, it's not good people VS bad people. It's not privileged people VS oppressed people. Instead, you're either in Jesus' pasture, or he's out looking for you. Joey needs to be reminded that love is a matter of truth *and* grace, and Zoë needs to be reminded that love is a matter of grace *and* truth.

Your role, as a parent of Joey and Zoë, is to disciple both of them to be missionaries for King Jesus.

A disciple of Jesus makes disciples who are missionaries for King Jesus.

ACTION STEPS

1. Read Matthew 5:13–16 and 5:43–48. The point of salt and light is that they are beneficial; they are good for people. Thus, we are supposed to do good works, deeds that are helpful, beneficial, and valuable. And we're supposed to do good for all people. What are some ways you can be a missionary to your neighbors and community by doing good deeds that glorify your Father in heaven?

2. Call to mind people you know across the political spectrum—people more on the left and people more on the right. Describe some specific ways that thinking like a missionary can change the way you view and interact with people on both sides of the political aisle.

21
HOW CAN CHRISTIANS NOT LOSE ON ELECTION DAY?

Wherever you live, an election day is likely on your horizon. In recent memory, each election year here in the U.S. seems to have grown in intensity and divisiveness. Is it possible for churches to position themselves in a way in which they cannot lose, regardless of the election outcome?

Wait. We cannot lose *regardless* of the election's outcome? Bad political policies don't just mean higher grocery prices or inconvenient red tape. They can generate oppression of minorities. They can sometimes cue forced starvations and ethnic cleansing. They can justify Maoist struggle sessions and Stalinist gulags. Bad legislation can condition people for switching labels on what's good and evil. Elections can set in motion tyrannical rule, religious persecution, and generational suffering. How can we suggest that churches can position themselves as unable to lose regardless of the outcome of an election?

Yet, this is not head-in-the-sand complacency. This is *hopefulness*, and it's the sum of **IT'S THE SUM OF CLEAR-HEADED CALCULATION.**

clear-headed calculation. And it's not guaranteed. The truth is, churches can lose their way sometimes, and election years multiply the needs to pull to the side and check the map. You basically need the rotating neck of an owl in order to see all the angles from which the losses can come. Sometimes the loss can come when churches get too cozy with political power. Other times, the loss can come from anti-Christian political policies which threaten to pummel the church until church people raise the white flag and surrender their convictions.

Sometimes the losses take time to see. A former missionary to Germany was telling me (Daniel) of how he witnessed the aftermath of the "tsunami" of secularist skepticism in Germany. The average German citizen knows very little about the Bible, yet as schoolchildren they were taught "negative higher criticism" of the Bible in public school. This creates a toxic environment for cultivating biblical convictions. Now back in the States, our friend is seeing the waves of biblical criticism hit here.

The more loudly the storm is raging, the more we can find a cheerful optimism sounding out-of-step and tone-deaf. And if each subsequent election is indeed the most important election of our lifetimes, shouldn't our tone in the church match the sobriety of the moment?

Yet there is a genuine, shining hopefulness that is the church's heritage even in pessimistic times. This Christian hopefulness is every bit as serious as the gravity of a historic election or as the tragedy of a country clawing itself apart. Christian hopefulness is for serious-minded grown-ups. It's characterized by *foresight, resilience, conviction,* and *logic.* And if the church is to win in Kingdom-work in an election year—come hell or high water—it's going to need

Christian hopefulness. How can we cultivate it in our lives, in our families, and in our churches?

THE FORESIGHT OF JOSEPH

Abraham's great grandson Joseph saved the Jewish clan from famine by being in the wrong place at the right time. His jealous brothers sold him into slavery after which he was taken to Egypt. Although it had looked like a tragedy of treachery, it turned out that Joseph was actually taken to Egypt by the mercy of God.

Through giving Joseph a series of prophetic dreams, God prepared Joseph to interpret others' dreams in Egypt. When the Pharaoh dreamt of seven fat cows being gobbled up by seven emaciated cows, Joseph explained that Egypt was about to have seven years of plenty followed by seven years of famine. In light of the coming famine, Joseph suggested a system of serious nationwide preparation.

The result? Because it stored grain over the years of plenty, Egypt had plenty to feed its people and sell to neighboring countries. When the famine hit Canaan, Joseph's brothers came to Egypt to buy provisions. It was at this time that Joseph recognized that his brothers had "intended to harm me, but God intended it for good to accomplish what is now being done, the saving of many lives" (Genesis 50:20).

Christian hopefulness sees God's mercy in years of plenty and famine alike. We see good times as seasons to prepare ourselves, and bad times as seasons to provide for others. In good times and bad, the church that keeps its trust firmly planted in God's mercy and provision cannot lose.

THE RESILIENCE OF DAVID

Reading through David's psalms is like taking multiple trips up and down a mountain. In one psalm, David sounds exuberant. The next, he sounds terrified. One day, he's bursting with gratitude. The next day, he's venting over God's inactivity.

David's disorderly ups and downs may look like a mismatch with the Sunday, dressed-up church crowd, but let's be honest: there's never been a more accurate description of the church from Monday to Saturday. Worshipful. Fearful. Grateful. Guilty.

The one regularity we can count on when reading the psalms is how a psalm is going to end. Whatever mood the psalmist starts with, the psalm regularly ends with a reaffirmation of trust in God.

THE PSALM REGULARLY ENDS WITH A REAFFIRMATION.

We as the church cannot lose if we find in whatever situation we are in a renewed reason to trust in God. Perhaps the situation calls us to gratitude for his blessings. Or perhaps it's a tough situation which confirms our dependence on him. He's our rock in scary situations, our redeemer in graceless situations, our wisdom in bewildering situations. Our trust in God is validated by whatever life throws our way. Christian hopefulness is resilient, regardless.

THE CONVICTION OF DANIEL

How do we know that the prophet Daniel was a man of deep conviction in God? We know because of *when* he prayed. He regularly prayed to God three times a day. There were times under the Babylonian King Nebuchadnezzar when devotion to God was looked down on, as well as times when it was intensely popular (as after God delivered Shadrach, Meshach, and Abednego from the fiery furnace). Fast forward into Daniel's life a few more years, and devotion to God was even more acceptable under the Medes. That is, until the king was manipulated into signing a decree that, for thirty days, no one in the empire could pray to anyone except the king.

Just as Daniel had prayed three times a day to God before the edict, he kept right on praying. On his knees, windows open, three times a day, there he was "giving thanks to his God, just as he had done before" (Daniel 6:10). For that, Daniel was thrown into a den of lions. A miracle of deliverance, a couple of dreams, and three chapters later, Daniel is back to praying—this time a prayer of repentance for his nation (Daniel 9:4–19).

Christian hopefulness keeps right on trusting God and practicing its convictions regardless of who is in power or what the law is.

It is true that convictional churches can lose a lot of things: political weight, cultural clout, financial benefits, and more. But with each fleeting thing the church loses, it is reminded of the eternal things it has always had which it cannot lose: the Word of God, the indwelling of the Spirit, the fellowship of believers, the hope of heaven. Is there even a comparison?

THE LOGIC OF PAUL

For Paul, persecution was not a hypothetical horizon depending on which Roman emperor might come next. Paul was already constantly in jail for his convictions. For fourteen years of Paul's ministry, the emperor was none other than the notorious Nero, and it was Nero who eventually had Paul beheaded.

So, we can safely assume that Paul wasn't sloganeering when he wrote, "For to me, to live is Christ and to die is gain " (Philippians 1:21). Neither option was metaphoric. And he really believed it: If he lived, great! If he died, great! He had the Lord's work to do if he lived, and he had the reality of heaven ahead. Either way, he could not lose. The church which trusts in God can say, "Either way," and follow it up with sincere reasons for hopefulness.

WHAT TIME IS IT?

Many of us experience everyday collisions between a younger optimism and an older sobriety that feeds on fearful headlines and stressful hypotheticals. What both our younger and older selves need isn't for one or the other to win. Rather, they both need to quiet themselves in the presence of a mentor who is older still. This mentor is the church of our forefathers and foremothers, who lived faithful lives during difficult times. It's the great "cloud of witnesses" who collectively urge us on, saying, "Christian, you can't lose!"

"Therefore, since we are surrounded by such a great cloud of witnesses, let us throw off everything that hinders and the sin that so easily entangles. And let us run with perseverance the race marked out for us, fixing our eyes on Jesus, the pioneer and perfecter of faith. For the joy set before him he endured the cross, scorning its shame, and sat down at the right hand of the throne of God." (Hebrews 12:1–2)

Christian hopefulness combines joy and suffering. It mingles the exuberance of faith with the seriousness of marathon-ready endurance.

A few years ago, I (Daniel) was asked to preach at the funeral of my spiritual grandmother. This was the woman who, with her husband, led my parents to know Jesus. To prepare for what I would say at the funeral, I asked her family if there were any sayings she was known for. One stuck out for its eccentricity and profundity. If someone asked her what time it was, she would answer, "It's time to serve the Lord."

Regardless of what happens in an election year, we *know* what time it is. It's time to serve the Lord.

May this conviction resound a hundred times more loudly than the pundits: *Come hell or high water, we who trust in God cannot lose.*

A disciple of Jesus can't lose.

ACTION STEPS

1. Read 1 Peter 3:13–17. What do you learn about being steadfast, resolute, and hopeful from this passage?

2. Which one of the four examples in this chapter seems most helpful to you right now? What can you do to imitate that example?

CONCLUSION

As we wrap up this book, we want to end with a crucial reminder for all of us who are disciples of Jesus. It's a reminder that is necessary for us because, although as disciples we know what we're about to say here is true, we have not always acted as though it is true, especially in the last few years.

Some of us have been driven by fear.

Some of us may be marked by anxiety about what will happen if so-and-so does or does not win the election.

Christians have acted out in anger and mean-spirited accusations toward those they disagree with, both unbelievers and brothers or sisters in Christ.

All of this suggests that maybe we have forgotten a very foundational truth. When it comes to following Jesus in a politically divided world, here's what we must never forget: *our hope is Jesus' kingdom.*

Our hope is not in the outcome of an election. It's not in who is in office. We do not look to Washington D.C. for a savior. As we noted at the outset of this book, "Our citizenship is heaven, and we look for a Savior from there, the Lord Jesus Christ" (Philippians 3:20).

So, while bad politics do real harm and bad policies cause real problems, and we do want to use whatever influence we might have to promote righteousness and justice, we don't place our hopes in politics. At least, we're not *supposed to*. When Christian people engage in angry attacks on their political "enemies," or when they give themselves over to fear and anxiety about the future of their country, they demonstrate that their hope is misplaced.

So, at the conclusion of this book, we must emphasize...

Our hope is in King Jesus, and nowhere else. And our core mission is to make disciples and to embody the values of Jesus' kingdom. We place our expectations for safety, security, and human flourishing not in the kingdoms of humanity, but in the kingdom of Jesus. And the means that King Jesus has given us of furthering his kingdom is by making disciples. He alone is the true hope for the world, and we get the honor of telling others (and retelling ourselves!) the best possible news: that Jesus is King.

APPENDIX A
VALUE STATEMENTS FROM THE GOSPEL OF MATTHEW

As previously referenced in chapter 11, this list aims to guide us in further contemplating Jesus' glory. This list compiles value statements we glean from the Gospel of Matthew. In each of these passages, Jesus models what should win over what in our value system. Again, just think of a game of rock, paper, scissors; Jesus is teaching us what's "rock" and what's "scissors."

3:13–15	Doing what is righteous over what makes most sense
4:1	Spirit-led over comfortable
4:3–4	Spiritual needs (e.g., our need for God's words) over physical comfort
4:5–10	Right way over easy way
4:18–19	Eternal needs over physical needs
5:11–12	Reward in heaven over comforts of earth
5:14–16	Being a light over blending in
5:20	Righteousness of the heart over technical obedience
5:23–24	Reconciliation over religious rituals

5:27–30   Heaven over pleasures of sin

5:32   Faithfulness in marriage over the easy way out

5:33–37   Doing what you say you'll do over making elaborate promises

5:38–42   The other person's salvation over your rights

5:43–48   Loving our enemies over just loving friends

6:1   Acts of righteousness for God over getting noticed by people

6:2–4   Reward in heaven over applause on earth

6:5–8   Authenticity in prayer over fancy words

6:16–18   Sincerity over putting on a show

6:19–21   Treasures in heaven over stuff of earth

6:24   Serving God over making money

6:25–34   Trust in God over worrying about stuff

6:26–27   Content in my worth over busying myself with worry

6:33   Seeking God's kingdom over meeting our needs

7:1–2   Showing mercy to others over mainly giving yourself mercy

7:3–5   Self-examination over always needing to fix other people's problems

7:7–8   Trusting in God's providence over keeping distance from God

7:12   Treating others the way you want to be treated over just treating yourself

7:13–14   Traveling the narrow path over settling for the easy path

7:15–20   Watching out for false prophets over complacently assuming the best

7:21–23   Doing our Father's will over doing impressive things for God

7:24–27   Following Jesus' teachings over just hearing Jesus' teachings

8:1–3   Showing mercy in personal ways over just helping from a distance

8:10–12   Having faith in Jesus' abilities over being born in the right group

8:19–22   The urgency of following Jesus over physical and family interests

8:24–26   Faith during a storm over panic during a storm

8:28–34   Helping the hurting over maintaining the peaceful status quo

9:1–8   Having our sins forgiven over being healed (the latter is confirmation of the former)

9:9–13   Hanging out with sinners over impressing the righteous

9:14–17   Celebrating Jesus' presence over maintaining old religious traditions

9:18–26   Our faith in Jesus' ability over our contentedness to leave Jesus alone

9:35–38   Compassion for the hurting (becoming a harvest worker) over living typical lives

10:14–15   Receptivity to Jesus' message over maintaining status quo

10:18–20   Confidence in Spirit's leading over avoidance of danger

10:21–22   Enduring to the end over chasing the approval of people

10:28   Fear of God over fear of persecutors

10:28–31   The peace of being known by God over fretting over persecution

10:32–33   Confessing Jesus before men over playing it safe

10:37   Loving Jesus more than loving the members of one's family

10:38–39 Losing our lives in Jesus over protecting our lives/lifestyles at all costs

10:40–42 Receiving Jesus' messengers over maintaining the status quo

11:2–6   Glorying in what God is doing in the world over needing God's personal intervention

11:16–19 Following Jesus and being vindicated over going along with cultural moods

11:25–26 Faith of a child over priding ourselves for being wise and intelligent

11:28–30 Resting in Jesus over shouldering it ourselves

12:1–8   Mercy (and recognizing people's needs) over sacrifice (and rigid adherence to rules and tradition)

12:11–12 Meeting a person's needs over taking care of your animal

12:13–21 Walking alongside the hurting over running over people

12:24–28 Recognizing Jesus' identity over maintaining status quo

12:38–42 Acknowledging Jesus' greatness over needing more signs from God

12:46–50 Your spiritual family of those who do God's will over your physical family

13:18–23 Bearing fruit over merely hearing the Word

13:24–30 Giving the unsaved more time over a strict separatism from the world

13:44–45 The kingdom of heaven over the stuff of earth

13:54–58 Trust in Jesus over judging him by physical standards ("Isn't this the carpenter's son?")

14:13–21 Meeting needs over one's own physical comfort

14:25–31 Courageous faith over calculated fear

15:1–3 Obeying God's commandments over keeping traditions

15:7–9 Heart for God over merely mouthing the right words

15:10–11 Watching our words (what comes out of our mouth, and heart) over watching our food (what comes into our mouths)

15:21–28 Persistent faith over leaving Jesus alone

15:32–38 Compassion for oppressed people over one's own physical comfort

16:1–4 Acknowledging Jesus' greatness over needing more signs

16:13–17 Recognizing Jesus as the Messiah and Son of God over respecting him as a great teacher

16:21–23 Following God's difficult plan over trying to prevent suffering

16:24–27 Denying ourselves over preserving our lifestyles

17:1–5 Listening to Jesus over mere prophets of God

17:14–20 Having faith in God over self-sufficiency

17:24–27 Doing as we're told (e.g., paying taxes) over unnecessarily offending

18:1–4 Humility of a child over "greatness"

18:6–9 Physical pain over spiritual stumbling/causing children to spiritually stumble

18:12 Seeking the stray over maintaining the flock

18:13–14 Rejoicing about the lost who's been found over being glad about the well-being of the flock

18:15–17 Confrontation and restoration of a fallen brother over letting him be

18:23–35 Forgiving as we've been forgiven over seeking justice when we've been wronged

19:3–6	Faithfulness and oneness in marriage over getting what we want
19:13–15	Welcoming children over maintaining serenity
19:16–22	Giving up what keeps you from following Jesus over maintaining a comfortable life
19:28–30	Leaving behind precious things for God's kingdom over maintaining a normal life
20:1–16	Thankful for being in God's kingdom over expecting preferential treatment
20:25–28	Serving people over lording it over people
20:30–34	Compassion for the hurting over ignoring needy people
21:12–13	Valuing holy things (e.g., the temple) as ways to connect with God over ways to make a profit
21:21–22	Faith without doubt over not bothering God
21:28–32	Unlikely believers over law-keeping unbelievers
21:33–44	Outsiders who bear the fruit of God's kingdom over the old guard who don't
22:1–10	Taking our King's invitation seriously over the treason of business as usual
22:15–21	Giving to God and government their due over confusing the two
22:37–39	Loving God over loving people
22:40	Love over more secondary commandments
23:5–12	Honoring God over amassing titles
23:11	Serving others over seeking greatness
23:15	Evangelizing people to a living faith over evangelizing people into a "faith" that doesn't transform you or them

23:16–22   Obligation to the things of God over obsession with the treasures of earth

23:23–24   Justice, mercy, and faithfulness (the weightier matters of the law) over tithing (lesser matters of the law)

23:25–28   Cleaning the "inside" (of greed, self-indulgence, hypocrisy, wickedness) over just cleaning the "outside"

23:37–39   Humbling ourselves before God's persistent and loving revelation over persistent hardheartedness

24:36–25:13 Readiness for Christ's coming over business as usual

25:14–30   Using what God has given us for his kingdom over living an inactive life

25:31–46   Feeding the hungry, giving drink to the thirsty, inviting the stranger, clothing the naked, visiting the sick and the prisoner (with an emphasis on doing this for Jesus' disciples) over keeping to ourselves

26:11   Recognizing Jesus' worth over other people's temporal needs

26:39   Doing God's will (even if it's sacrifice) over doing our will

26:51–52   The way of peace over the way of the sword

28:10   Spreading God's good news over fearful inaction

28:18–20   Making disciples over a life of lesser pursuits

APPENDIX B
RACISM AND THE GOSPEL

Bowling looks easier than it is. It's true that there's a fairly wide lane to roll the ball in order to knock down the pins. All we have to do is avoid the gutters, and we'll accomplish something. Yet even though the gutters are narrow and the lane is wide, somehow the bowling ball can easily end up in one gutter or the other.

Similarly, the same can go for speaking out as a Christian on the issue of racism. It looks a lot easier than it is. It's almost as if our voices are metallic and the gutters are magnetized.

One gutter corrupts us. The other gutter co-opts us. Although there is an entire lane of amazing progress that Christians can get accomplished, we tend to glide toward the gutters and drop out of effectiveness—this at a time when a bleeding society needs the gospel's implications most urgently.

THE LANE

First, let's look at the lane. The good news is that Jesus has given the church the tools we need

JESUS HAS GIVEN THE CHURCH THE TOOLS WE NEED.

to address tribalistic attitudes and actions—whether white versus black, Jew versus Arab, or any other racial tension.

For one thing, Jesus gave us the tool of open, honest conversation with people who are different from us. Jesus models in-depth conversations—first with a Jewish Sanhedrin member, then with a Samaritan outcast. He's eating at the home of a hated tax collector, and then at the home of a professional holy man, a Pharisee.

Consider all the tools Jesus has given us to bring repentance and reconciliation and to heal the lacerations of racial tribalism.

- He teaches us how to have compassion for those who are hurting: "But a Samaritan, as he traveled, came where the [wounded Jewish] man was; and when he saw him, he took pity on him" (Luke 10:33).
- He teaches us how to lament: "As he approached Jerusalem and saw the city, he wept over it" (Luke 19:41).
- He teaches us how to repent: "Repent, for the kingdom of heaven has come near" (Matthew 4:17).
- He teaches us how to reconcile with people whom we might have hurt: "First go and be reconciled to them" (Matthew 5:24a).
- He teaches us to seek justice for the oppressed: "He has sent me. . . to set the oppressed free" (Luke 4:18b).

• He teaches us how to bring people together who would naturally hate each other: for example, Jesus brought into his band of twelve both Simon the Zealot (who hated Roman oppression) and Matthew the tax collector (who benefited from Roman oppression).

• He teaches us how to view each other this side of the cross: "Here there is no Gentile or Jew, circumcised or uncircumcised, barbarian, Scythian, slave or free, but Christ is all, and is in all" (Colossians 3:11).

The church has been given the tools that are needed for healing racial hurt. The church can lead the way in repentant and compassionate reconciliation. We can model humble conversation from the posture of a learner. We can intentionally seek to build the kind of churches that look like Revelation 7:9:

> "After this I looked, and there before me was a great multitude that no one could count, from every nation, tribe, people and language, standing before the throne and before the Lamb." (Revelation 7:9a)

As Christians, we have so much to offer a hurting world, yet the lane seems all too often greased in favor of the gutters.

A GUTTER THAT CORRUPTS ME

The first gutter corrupts us with the wrong kind of comfort. This is a blinded comfort that says, "Racism can't still be a problem.

After all, we had the Civil Rights Movement. And even if it still is a problem, it can't be that big of a problem. It's not affecting me anyway."

This is a comfort borne out of ignorance or apathy when it comes to the concerns of people who are different from us. Depending on which category you belong to, it can be easy to put the interests of urban, suburban, or rural people completely out of mind.

Unbothered by the interests of others, we can become consumed with the concerns of our own. We fixate on the politicians who make our particular demographic feel more important than others.

A GUTTER THAT CO-OPTS ME

The other gutter co-opts us with the wrong kind of conflict. There are voices and organizations in racial debates which will try to enlist us in a vicious battle between the oppressors and the oppressed, as if we could cleanly separate humans into one category or the other.

The method is to divide humans into subgroups according to factors such as race, sexual orientation, gender, religion, and economic status. Accordingly, you could be perceived either as an oppressed person whose voice matters, or as an oppressive, privileged person who should feel perpetually sheepish and stay quiet. (This has become the default ethical system of "progressivism," or more specifically, of "intersectional feminism"; for more information on this, refer back to chapter 5.)

If you want to cultivate true racial reconciliation, then you will not want to allow yourself to be enlisted in the battle the way progressivism draws the lines. For if, in addressing racism, you take your cues from progressive voices, you will likely be shamed, discredited, and canceled until you go all the way. All the way into what? Here are some examples of action steps which a well-meaning Christian can be forced to take in the name of fighting oppression, once they let progressivism frame their thinking:

- If you want to fight oppression, you must see free-market capitalism as inherently racist.
- If you want to fight oppression, you must oppose the gender binary as inherently oppressive.
- If you want to fight oppression, you must denounce America as systematically white supremacist.
- If you want to fight oppression, you must fully support LGBTQIA ethics as an ally.
- If you want to fight oppression, you must support access to abortion as reproductive justice.
- If you want to fight oppression, you must resist the cultural influence of numerous Christian beliefs.

If you are not careful, your compassion will be co-opted by an ethical system that claims to help

YOUR COMPASSION WILL BE CO-OPTED.

the oppressed, but which does not acknowledge the real character of God, who created all of humanity in his image. This ethical system is more about a reversal of power than about reconciling humans with God and with each other. As Christians, we should want to pursue repentance and reconciliation, not revolution.

CONCLUSION

As a Christian in volatile times, you will be pressured to be corrupted by comfort. In such times, remember that we will be judged by Jesus as to how well we have treated our brothers and sisters who were considered "the least of these" (Matthew 25:31–46).

You will also be pressured to be co-opted by the wrong kind of conflict. In such times, remember that the church has been given tools far more transformational than any arsenal a secular culture can offer.

Either gutter tries to gut the gospel of its power.

What if instead we use the lane, without drifting into the gutters, and bring people together in the name of Jesus?

APPENDIX C
A CAUTION

In chapter 6, we described four models for how church and state have interacted throughout history, from synthesis to strict opposition. Again, here's what we described:

- **(S) Synthesis** – An S has two semi-circles that look like each other and blend into each other. What we're calling S-level interaction is close interaction between church and state, such that there is a synthesis of sorts between the two. For example, especially in its medieval years, the Roman Catholic Church experienced a synthesis of church and state. During these years, church and state were closely allied while each carried out an important, distinct role for society. This view was articulated by Catholic theologian Thomas Aquinas.
- **(C) Conversion** – The letter C helps us picture a change, a transformation. The shape of C suggests a turn ahead. Thus, the C stands for "conversion." John Calvin taught that the state is a gift from God and that the church can help convert/

transform it so that what has been corrupted can be made godlier and more just. Abraham Kuyper, Calvinist and onetime Prime Minister of the Netherlands, famously said, "There is not a square inch in the whole domain of our human existence over which Christ, who is Sovereign over all, does not cry, Mine!"[33] Thus, the church can and should seek to transform all layers of society on behalf of Christ.

• **(T) Tension** – In a T, you see two sides divided by a solid line. In a T, both sides kind of do their own thing, and there's not a lot of interaction between them. A T-model church-state interaction is going to stand for the word "tension." Martin Luther taught that there is a necessary, ongoing tension between the church and the state. God has given one set of ethics to the church (with priority given to grace) and another to the state (with priority given to justice). It is permissible for Christians to be involved in government, but the distinction between the two needs to be kept clear.

• **(O) Opposition** – Notice how an O is sealed off from the outside. It suggests a strict separation between what's inside and what's outside. In this way, for example, Anabaptists emphasized a sharp, impassable division between the values of the church and the state. It is better for the church and its members not to get involved in governmental affairs (e.g., military service, state jobs, etc.); even voting may be discouraged.

---

[33] James D. Bratt, Ed, *Abraham Kuyper: A Centennial Reader* (Grand Rapids: William B. Eerdmans Publishing Company, 1998), 461.

Historically speaking, each level of interaction fit with a particular governing body's reception given to the church at the time. That being the case, let's explore a hypothetical. What if a path opens in your country for greater church-state interaction? Let's say that increasing numbers of people are sensing moral chaos and want to see the country's leaders acknowledge (or re-acknowledge) Christian principles in their legislation. Or let's say that perhaps a crucial voting bloc is feeling nostalgia for a time when there was more of a Christian consensus reflected in the government, and as a result, the synthesis model is growing in popularity.

If more and more people in your country desired a church-state synthesis, should you see this an opportunity—or a temptation?

SHOULD YOU SEE THIS AN OPPORTUNITY—OR A TEMPTATION?

That's a tough question. On the one hand, the Roman Empire was made far more humane when Christian convictions and values, such as the ones outlined in chapter 3, began being implemented. On the other hand, state-and-church alliances have resulted in some hideous abuses of power. Inquisitions. Pogroms. Crusader violence. Expulsion of Jews from entire countries.

Let's be clear: societies lose when uninfluenced by Christianity. We would be naïve to think that, for example, a country can retain the importance of forgiveness when wronged, care for the marginalized, and the sacredness of all human life very long after its people has stopped holding Christian convictions. Although the American Declaration of Independence calls human equality "self-evident," nothing could be further from the truth. The equality of all humans is not a self-evident truth; it's a *Christian* truth which seemed self-evident to the signers of the Declaration because they were steeped in Christian principles.

Yet the purpose of this appendix is to give voice to a caution that can get drowned out in many Christians' eagerness to "take back this country for God." Yes, societies lose when uninfluenced by Christianity. But Christians can also lose important characteristics when it comes to church-state alliances. This appendix should not be read as an argument advocating or denouncing a particular model of church-state interaction. It should be read as a caution: the more political power a church enjoys, the more susceptible it becomes to significant losses.

In this appendix, we will look at four such losses. The backdrop of these four losses is the story of how the Roman emperor Constantine converted to Christianity and began to convert the empire to Christianity. What you'll read below is a warning against the tendency of Christians to trust politics to give Christians what God alone can give, and to do for the church what God alone can do (Matthew 7:6).

#1 – LOSING OUR KINSHIP WITH MARGINALIZATION

Christianity was born into a world that did not know what to do with it. Christianity was sort of Jewish (Jesus was a Jew, after all), but it was often met by persecution from Jewish religious leaders who wanted nothing to do with it. It was also somewhat of a Gentile thing because Jesus set the church up to bring together Jews and Gentiles. Yet early Christians found themselves persecuted by Gentile leaders too, notably Roman emperors such as Nero, Domitian, and Diocletian. Christians found themselves often marginalized in multiple contexts.

And then, a massive shift of cultural winds shocked everyone in the 300s. Although not a Christian prior to this event, Roman Emperor Constantine credited Jesus with helping him win the decisive battle that made him emperor. This was in the year A.D. 312, and the next year, Constantine signed the Edict of Milan, granting religious freedom to Christians.

Many church leaders rushed headlong into the new arrangement, seeing their newfound imperial favor as an obvious gift from God. Now, there's a sense in which the arrangement was an obvious gift to the empire. How can we be anything but grateful for the care that society's throwaways finally began to receive as hospitals and orphanages, nursing homes and mental asylums began springing up throughout the empire in the A.D. 300s and 400s? Yet the arrangement would prove to be a mixed blessing for the church, as its apparent gains were balanced by some serious losses.

The first loss we must watch out for is when many Christians lost their connection to marginalized people. This loss became especially possible after A.D. 380, when Christianity was made the official religion of the Roman Empire.

The once-persecuted were now in danger of becoming the persecutor. It was increasingly easy to forget that the roles were only recently switched. Had the church forgotten how it felt to be wronged? Instead of inviting outsiders into their community with grace and truth, Christians in power eventually kept tightening the screws on non-Christians until they had to comply. By the end of the fourth century, Emperor Theodosius had prohibited non-Christians from worshiping in public (their temples were destroyed anyway) or in private. In the end, people had to convert to Christianity, or else.

Any who balked at Theodosius's requirement to "practice the religion which the divine Peter the Apostle transmitted to the Romans" were "demented and insane," self-designated for "divine vengeance," and subject to "retribution of Our own initiative." Theodosius went on to make his own questionable assumption officially unquestionable: this state-sponsored violence "we shall assume in accordance with divine judgment."[34]

A much more accurate assumption would have been that Jesus wanted his church to *love* outsiders , like he said. The problem is these outsiders had gone from being lost sheep to being political enemies.

> ## JESUS WANTED HIS CHURCH TO LOVE OUTSIDERS.

#2 – LOSING OUR COURAGE FOR DENUNCIATION

The people of God have often been commissioned by God to speak unfashionable truth to unjust rulers. Nathan tells David, "You are the man!" (2 Samuel 12:7), Micah denounces the rulers of Israel for hating good and loving evil (Micah 3:1–2), and Stephen calls the Sanhedrin the betrayers and murderers of Jesus (Acts 7:52).

It is very difficult to carry out such critique while perched atop the branch of imperial blessedness. What naturally comes out instead are compliments: Eusebius speaking of Constantine as the "blessed

---

[34] Bruce L. Shelley, *Church History in Plain Language,* 2nd ed. (Nashville: Thomas Nelson Publishers, 1995), 96–97.

one" and "friend of God"[35] with "sacred head,"[36] "majestic dignity," and "invincible strength and vigor."[37] Somehow, neither the emperor's vengeful temperament nor any other vice makes the cut in Eusebius's biography of Constantine.[38]

Of course, denunciations came, but primarily against the other party. Constantine's rival in the East was clearly the "enemy of God," "hopelessly debased," with "worthless character."[39] According to Athanasius, the Arian emperor Constantius was unquestionably worse than King Saul, King Ahab, and Pontius Pilate and was doubtless a forerunner of the Antichrist.[40] It is ironically similar to if one were reading Fox's take on a Democratic president or CNN's take on a Republican president.

And when governmental leaders who favored Christianity did, in fact, receive criticism from the church, it usually worked out because of the church's increasing ability to intimidate. One example is the famous excommunication of Emperor Theodosius by Bishop Ambrose. Emperor Theodosius had slaughtered 7,000 citizens because of a grievance, and Ambrose refused him communion until Theodosius finally repented.[41]

The early church refused to be divided into the typical categories (Jew or Gentile, Roman or Greek, etc.). This refusal led

---

[35] Eusebius, "Chapter 52," *Life of Constantine: Book I*, trans. Ernest Cushing Richardson, from Nicene and Post-Nicene Fathers, Second Series, vol. 1, ed. Philip Schaff and Henry Wace (Buffalo: Christian Literature Publishing, 1890), ed. for New Advent by Kevin Knight, http://www.newadvent.org/fathers/25021.htm.

[36] Eusebius, "Chapter 1," *Life of Constantine: Book I*.

[37] Eusebius, "Chapter 10," *Life of Constantine: Book III*, trans. Ernest Cushing Richardson, from *Nicene and Post-Nicene Fathers, Second Series, vol. 1*, ed. Philip Schaff and Henry Wace (Buffalo: Christian Literature Publishing, 1890), ed. for *New Advent* by Kevin Knight, http://www.newadvent.org/fathers/25023.htm.

[38] Justo L. Gonzalez, *The Story of Christian: the Early Church to the Dawn of the Reformation*, vol. 1 (New York: HarperOne, 2014), Kindle edition.

[39] Eusebius, "Chapter 52," *Life of Constantine: Book I*.

[40] Richard A. Todd, "Constantine and the Christian Empire," in *Introduction to the History of Christianity*, ed. Tim Dowley (Minneapolis: Fortress Press, 2002), 146.

[41] Shelley, 98.

a mocker of Christianity to call it a "Third Race." As sociologist Os Guinness puts it, the insult became an insight.[42] As a "Third Race," the church can offer (and receive) critique and remain unafraid of endangering its privileged political position. When the church subsumes itself under particular parties in exchange for a voice at the table, we know what often happens to that voice once it gets there.

#3 – LOSING OUR RESISTANCE TO INFILTRATION

So long as neither the church nor the empire felt interfered with, the church of the 300s never sensed the infiltration that was taking place. Emperor Constantine and the church wanted the same things . . . didn't they?

Actually, having interests that merge for a season is not the same as desiring the same things. Constantine, above all, desired *unity*.[43] And, as the sole emperor of an unstable empire glued together with fragile common interests, why shouldn't he? The Roman emperor had always been the head of the state religion and, as such, was concerned to keep peace between the people and the gods.

For a season, Constantine's driving motivation paralleled the interests of the church. Yet it is the nature of power to extend as far as it is able. In the expansion, the state's overriding priorities cannot help but pull at the church to become

IT IS THE NATURE OF POWER TO EXTEND.

---

[42] Os Guinness, *The Dust of Death* (Downers Grove: Inter-Varsity Christian Fellowship, 1973), 368.

[43] Constantine "delighted in a general harmony of sentiment, while he regarded the unyielding wills with aversion." See Eusebius, "Chapter 44," *Life of Constantine: Book I.* His intentions in working with the church were to establish "a common harmony of sentiment among all the servants of God." See Eusebius, "Chapter 65," *Life of Constantine: Book II,* trans. Ernest Cushing Richardson, from *Nicene and Post-Nicene Fathers, Second Series, vol. 1,* ed. Philip Schaff and Henry Wace (Buffalo: Christian Literature Publishing, 1890), ed. for *New Advent* by Kevin Knight, http://www.newadvent.org/fathers/25022.htm. In his estimation, "intestine strife within the Church of God, is far more evil and dangerous than any kind of war or conflict." See Eusebius, "Chapter 12," *Life of Constantine: Book III.*

something else over time. No stranger to power politics, Chuck Colson, former Special Counsel to President Richard Nixon, wrote,

> "Governments, with rare exceptions, seek to expand their power beyond the mandate to restrain evil, preserve order, and promote justice. Most often they do this by venturing into religious or moral areas. The reason is twofold: the state needs religious legitimization for its policies and an independent church is the one structure that rivals the state's claim for ultimate allegiance."[44]

When the church aligns with those in power and gets lulled into forgetfulness, it loses its resistance to infiltration. The church-state relationship can start out so smoothly that the church does not even realize it is being infiltrated. But, when one side values unity over orthodoxy, then sometimes it makes sense to them to begin sanding down orthodoxy's sharp edges to achieve unity (such as when Constantine's son Constantius tried to forcibly convert the bishops to Arianism).

#4 – LOSING OUR UNIQUENESS IN DURATION

A church that ties itself to a regime at the summit has tied itself to a future avalanche. Rome fell. All earthly kingdoms crumble sooner or later. The bishop who decided it would be expedient to switch his affiliation to Arianism and keep his job found himself not only on the

---

[44] Charles Colson, *God and Government: An Insider's View on the Boundaries between Faith and Politics* (Grand Rapids: Zondervan, 2007), 128.

wrong side of orthodoxy (all that really matters), but quite surprisingly on the wrong side of history as well. Who knew? Jesus built a kingdom that would outlast every regime.

> "Then the iron, the clay, the bronze, the silver, and the gold were all broken to pieces and became like chaff on a threshing floor in the summer. The wind swept them away without leaving a trace. But the rock that struck the statue became a huge mountain and filled the whole earth." (Daniel 2:35, ESV)

And no, the rock was not Constantine. Contrary to what Eusebius and his fellow Christians believed at the time, Constantine's empire filled only a fraction of the earth, and Rome would fall less than two hundred years later, only a fraction of the church's age.

If there's a single bullseye belief that characterizes a church that endures, it's that Jesus alone is the saving, risen king. And Jesus' kingdom lasts on into eternity. It's the only thing in this world "that cannot be shaken" (Hebrews 12:28). Eternal duration is something tragic to barter away, given that no earthly kingdom has anything nearly as valuable to offer in return.

ABOUT THE AUTHORS

JOHN WHITTAKER (DMin, Gordon-Conwell Theological Seminary) is a Bible teacher whose goal is to provide "blue jeans theology—theology for everyday life. He is the creator of The Listener's Commentary on the New Testament, author of *Bible in Life*, and has served full- and part-time as professor at Boise Bible College.

DANIEL MCCOY (PhD, North-West University) is the editorial director of Renew.org. He is also a philosophy professor-at-large for Ozark Christian College. Among his books are *The Popular Handbook of World Religions* (general editor) and *Real Life Theology* (co-general editor with Bobby Harrington). He and his wife have five kids.